DEEP LEARNING FOR BEGINNERS

Neural Networks, NLP, and Vision with
TensorFlow and Keras

THOMPSON CARTER

TABLE OF CONTENTS

INTRODUCTION..**11**

DEEP LEARNING FOR BEGINNERS: NEURAL NETWORKS, NLP, AND VISION WITH TENSORFLOW AND KERAS......................................11

1. WHAT IS DEEP LEARNING?..11

2. THE ROLE OF TENSORFLOW AND KERAS......................................14

3. WHY THIS BOOK?...15

4. REAL-WORLD APPLICATIONS OF DEEP LEARNING.........................16

5. HOW TO USE THIS BOOK 17

6. THE JOURNEY AHEAD..18

CHAPTER 1: INTRODUCTION TO DEEP LEARNING.............**20**

1.1 OVERVIEW OF DEEP LEARNING AND ITS IMPACT ON MODERN TECHNOLOGY..20

1.2 KEY CONCEPTS: ARTIFICIAL INTELLIGENCE, MACHINE LEARNING, AND DEEP LEARNING 21

1.3 WHY USE TENSORFLOW AND KERAS FOR DEEP LEARNING? 23

1.4 SETTING UP THE ENVIRONMENT...24

1.5 A "HELLO WORLD" EXAMPLE: PREDICTING SIMPLE DATA TRENDS 25

EXPLANATION OF THE MODEL 27

CHAPTER 2: UNDERSTANDING NEURAL NETWORKS **29**

2.1 THE STRUCTURE OF NEURAL NETWORKS 29

2.2 HOW NEURAL NETWORKS LEARN..31

2.3 KEY TERMINOLOGIES 32

2.4 REAL-WORLD EXAMPLE: PREDICTING HOUSE PRICES.......................33

EXPLANATION OF THE EXAMPLE...36

CHAPTER 3: WORKING WITH TENSORFLOW AND KERAS ..38

3.1 INTRODUCTION TO TENSORFLOW...38

3.2 KERAS: A HIGH-LEVEL API FOR TENSORFLOW 40

3.3 BUILDING, COMPILING, AND TRAINING A NEURAL NETWORK WITH

KERAS...41

3.4 REAL-WORLD EXAMPLE: SPAM DETECTION 43

EXPLANATION OF SPAM DETECTION EXAMPLE.............................46

CHAPTER 4: DATA PREPROCESSING FOR DEEP LEARNING

....**48**

4.1 IMPORTANCE OF CLEAN AND NORMALIZED DATA.................48

4.2 TECHNIQUES FOR DATA PREPROCESSING...............................49

4.3 PREPARING DATASETS FOR DEEP LEARNING 52

4.4 REAL-WORLD EXAMPLE: PREPROCESSING A DATASET FOR

PREDICTING CUSTOMER CHURN...54

BENEFITS OF PREPROCESSING..57

CHAPTER 5: ACTIVATION FUNCTIONS 58

5.1 WHAT ARE ACTIVATION FUNCTIONS AND WHY ARE THEY

IMPORTANT?..58

5.2 Popular Activation Functions...59

5.3 Choosing the Right Activation Function for Your Task......65

5.4 Visualizing Activation Functions and Their Impact..............67

CHAPTER 6: TRAINING DEEP NEURAL NETWORKS............70

6.1 Loss Functions 70

6.2 Optimization Algorithms...72

6.3 Training Parameters 74

6.4 Real-World Example: Training a Network to Predict Loan

Defaults 75

Analysis of Results 78

CHAPTER 7: AVOIDING OVERFITTING AND

UNDERFITTING..80

7.1 Concepts of Overfitting and Underfitting 80

7.2 Techniques to Prevent Overfitting...82

7.3 Evaluating Model Performance 84

7.4 Real-World Example: Improving the Accuracy of a

Classification Model..86

CHAPTER 8: CONVOLUTIONAL NEURAL NETWORKS (CNNS)

..91

8.1 Understanding CNNs for Image Processing Tasks..................91

8.2 Key Components of CNNs 92

8.3 Building Your First CNN with Keras...94

8.4 REAL-WORLD EXAMPLE: RECOGNIZING HANDWRITTEN DIGITS 96

ANALYSIS OF RESULTS 98

CHAPTER 9: ADVANCED CNN ARCHITECTURES 100

9.1 OVERVIEW OF POPULAR ARCHITECTURES 100

9.2 TRANSFER LEARNING...103

9.3 FINE-TUNING CNNS 104

9.4 REAL-WORLD EXAMPLE: CLASSIFYING IMAGES USING A PRE-
TRAINED RESNET MODEL 104

RESULTS AND ANALYSIS..109

CHAPTER 10: NATURAL LANGUAGE PROCESSING (NLP)

BASICS 110

10.1 INTRODUCTION TO NLP AND ITS IMPORTANCE IN AI......................110

10.2 TEXT PREPROCESSING 111

10.3 REPRESENTING TEXT AS NUMBERS 114

10.4 REAL-WORLD EXAMPLE: SENTIMENT ANALYSIS ON CUSTOMER

REVIEWS 116

CHAPTER 11: RECURRENT NEURAL NETWORKS (RNNS) ..120

11.1 UNDERSTANDING SEQUENTIAL DATA AND WHY RNNS ARE USED

....120

11.2 KEY CONCEPTS OF RNNS 121

11.3 BUILDING AND TRAINING RNNS WITH TENSORFLOW AND KERAS

....122

11.4 REAL-WORLD EXAMPLE: PREDICTING STOCK PRICES USING RNNS
.... 125

ANALYSIS OF RESULTS 129

CHAPTER 12: LONG SHORT-TERM MEMORY (LSTM) AND
GRU **130**

12.1 LIMITATIONS OF RNNS AND HOW LSTMS AND GRUS SOLVE THEM
.... 130

12.2 COMPONENTS OF LSTMS 131

12.3 GRUS: A SIMPLER ALTERNATIVE 133

12.4 CHOOSING BETWEEN LSTMS AND GRUS 133

12.5 REAL-WORLD EXAMPLE: GENERATING TEXT USING LSTMS 134

EXPECTED OUTPUT 138

ANALYSIS OF RESULTS 138

CHAPTER 13: ATTENTION MECHANISMS AND
TRANSFORMERS **139**

13.1 UNDERSTANDING ATTENTION IN DEEP LEARNING 139

13.2 THE ROLE OF TRANSFORMERS IN NLP AND BEYOND 141

13.3 INTRODUCTION TO BERT AND GPT ARCHITECTURES 142

13.4 REAL-WORLD EXAMPLE: TEXT SUMMARIZATION USING
TRANSFORMERS 143

13.5 APPLICATIONS OF TRANSFORMERS BEYOND NLP 146

CHAPTER 14: WORKING WITH IMAGES IN DEEP LEARNING
....**148**

14.1 DATA AUGMENTATION..148

14.2 PREPARING IMAGE DATASETS FOR DEEP LEARNING.......................151

14.3 REAL-WORLD EXAMPLE: BUILDING AN IMAGE CLASSIFIER FOR
DETECTING PLANT DISEASES 152

ANALYSIS OF RESULTS..157

CHAPTER 15: OBJECT DETECTION WITH DEEP LEARNING
...158

15.1 UNDERSTANDING OBJECT DETECTION 158

15.2 POPULAR OBJECT DETECTION MODELS 159

15.3 BUILDING AN OBJECT DETECTION PIPELINE 160

15.4 REAL-WORLD EXAMPLE: DETECTING TRAFFIC SIGNS IN REAL-TIME
....162

15.5 ANALYSIS AND INSIGHTS 166

CHAPTER 16: GENERATIVE ADVERSARIAL NETWORKS
(GANS) 168

16.1 INTRODUCTION TO GANS: GENERATORS AND DISCRIMINATORS .168

16.2 APPLICATIONS OF GANS..169

16.3 BUILDING A SIMPLE GAN WITH TENSORFLOW 170

16.4 REAL-WORLD EXAMPLE: GENERATING SYNTHETIC IMAGES FOR
DATA AUGMENTATION..175

16.5 ANALYSIS AND INSIGHTS 177

CHAPTER 17: AUTOENCODERS AND DIMENSIONALITY
REDUCTION 179

17.1 UNDERSTANDING AUTOENCODERS AND THEIR USE CASES 179

17.2 REDUCING DIMENSIONS FOR VISUALIZATION AND FEATURE EXTRACTION 181

17.3 REAL-WORLD EXAMPLE: USING AUTOENCODERS FOR ANOMALY DETECTION IN FINANCIAL TRANSACTIONS..................................182

ANALYSIS AND INSIGHTS 186

CHAPTER 18: HYPERPARAMETER TUNING 188

18.1 IMPORTANCE OF HYPERPARAMETER TUNING IN DEEP LEARNING188

18.2 METHODS FOR HYPERPARAMETER TUNING 189

18.3 AUTOMATING TUNING WITH KERAS TUNER 193

18.4 REAL-WORLD EXAMPLE: FINDING THE BEST MODEL FOR PREDICTING DIABETES 194

18.5 ANALYSIS AND INSIGHTS 197

CHAPTER 19: EVALUATING AND DEPLOYING DEEP LEARNING MODELS...199

19.1 METRICS FOR CLASSIFICATION, REGRESSION, AND RANKING 199

19.2 EXPORTING AND DEPLOYING MODELS.............................203

19.3 REAL-WORLD EXAMPLE: DEPLOYING A TENSORFLOW MODEL AS A WEB API 204

19.4 ANALYSIS AND INSIGHTS 207

CHAPTER 20: SCALING DEEP LEARNING WITH CLOUD COMPUTING 209

20.1 USING CLOUD PLATFORMS FOR TRAINING MODELS 209

20.2 DISTRIBUTED TRAINING WITH TENSORFLOW 211

20.3 REAL-WORLD EXAMPLE: TRAINING A LARGE-SCALE NLP MODEL

IN THE CLOUD 213

20.4 ANALYSIS AND INSIGHTS 216

CHAPTER 21: ETHICS AND CHALLENGES IN DEEP

LEARNING **218**

21.1 BIAS IN DEEP LEARNING MODELS AND WAYS TO MITIGATE IT 218

21.2 EXPLAINABILITY AND INTERPRETABILITY OF DEEP LEARNING

MODELS 220

21.3 CHALLENGES IN DEEP LEARNING 222

21.4 CASE STUDY: ENSURING FAIRNESS IN LOAN APPROVAL MODELS

....223

21.5 ANALYSIS AND INSIGHTS 226

CHAPTER 22: FUTURE DIRECTIONS IN DEEP LEARNING 228

22.1 EMERGING TRENDS IN DEEP LEARNING 228

22.2 QUANTUM COMPUTING AND ITS IMPACT ON DEEP LEARNING 230

22.3 TIPS FOR STAYING UPDATED IN THE FIELD 231

22.4 FINAL PROJECT: BUILDING A COMPLETE NLP OR VISION SYSTEM

....233

22.5 ANALYSIS AND INSIGHTS 236

INTRODUCTION

Deep Learning for Beginners: Neural Networks, NLP, and Vision with TensorFlow and Keras

Deep learning has become one of the most transformative technologies in the modern era, powering everything from virtual assistants to medical diagnostics. With its ability to model complex patterns in large datasets, deep learning enables machines to perform tasks previously thought to be exclusive to human intelligence—like understanding natural language, recognizing images, and even generating creative content. This book, *Deep Learning for Beginners: Neural Networks, NLP, and Vision with TensorFlow and Keras,* is designed to make deep learning accessible to those just starting their journey, with a focus on practical applications and real-world examples.

This introduction lays the foundation for what you will learn in the book, providing a high-level overview of deep learning, its relationship to artificial intelligence and machine learning, and the tools and frameworks that make it possible for beginners to get started. We'll also discuss the real-world impact of deep learning and why it's important to understand its principles and applications.

1. What is Deep Learning?

1.1 Deep Learning as a Subset of AI

Deep learning is a specialized field within artificial intelligence (AI) and machine learning (ML). While AI aims to create systems capable of performing tasks that normally require human intelligence, ML focuses on teaching machines to learn from data rather than being explicitly programmed. Deep learning takes this a step further, leveraging artificial neural networks to automatically discover patterns and representations in data.

For example:

- Traditional programming involves explicitly coding rules and logic for a specific task.
- Machine learning allows models to learn patterns by analyzing labeled data (e.g., identifying spam emails).
- Deep learning, powered by neural networks, can identify complex features in unstructured data like images and text, enabling applications such as facial recognition and language translation.

1.2 Key Characteristics of Deep Learning

Deep learning stands out from traditional ML techniques because of its ability to:

1. **Handle Unstructured Data**:
   o Works seamlessly with text, images, videos, and audio.

- o Applications: Sentiment analysis, image classification, and speech recognition.

2. **Learn Hierarchical Representations**:
   - o Neural networks extract features at multiple levels, such as edges, shapes, and objects in images.
   - o Applications: Object detection, facial recognition.

3. **Scale with Data and Compute Power**:
   - o Performance improves with more data and faster hardware (GPUs, TPUs).
   - o Applications: Training large language models like GPT and BERT.

1.3 Why Deep Learning Matters

Deep learning has revolutionized industries by achieving superhuman performance in some areas:

- **Healthcare**: Detecting diseases like cancer from medical images.
- **Finance**: Predicting stock trends and detecting fraudulent transactions.
- **Retail**: Powering recommendation systems that personalize shopping experiences.
- **Entertainment**: Enabling AI-driven content creation like image generation and text synthesis.

These real-world applications make deep learning a critical skill for developers, data scientists, and engineers.

2. The Role of TensorFlow and Keras

2.1 What is TensorFlow?

TensorFlow is an open-source machine learning framework developed by Google. It provides a robust, scalable platform for implementing machine learning and deep learning models. TensorFlow supports:

- **Efficient Computation**: Optimized for GPU/TPU acceleration.
- **Scalability**: Ideal for small experiments and large-scale deployments.
- **Flexibility**: Low-level APIs for fine-grained control over model development.

2.2 What is Keras?

Keras is a high-level API for TensorFlow that simplifies the process of building deep learning models. It abstracts the complexities of TensorFlow, making it beginner-friendly while still powerful for advanced use cases.

Advantages of Keras:

1. **Ease of Use**: Simple syntax for rapid prototyping.

2. **Prebuilt Components**: Ready-to-use layers, optimizers, and loss functions.

3. **Modularity**: Highly customizable models with minimal effort.

For example, creating a basic neural network with Keras can be done in a few lines of code, making it an excellent starting point for beginners.

3. Why This Book?

3.1 Bridging the Gap Between Theory and Practice

Many resources on deep learning are either too theoretical or assume advanced expertise in mathematics and programming. This book aims to fill that gap by:

- Providing jargon-free explanations of concepts.
- Demonstrating real-world use cases for deep learning.
- Offering hands-on tutorials using TensorFlow and Keras.

3.2 Structured Learning Path

The book is divided into three major parts:

1. **Neural Networks**: Fundamentals of building and training neural networks.

2. **Natural Language Processing (NLP)**: Using deep learning to process and analyze text.

3. **Computer Vision**: Applying convolutional neural networks (CNNs) to interpret images and videos.

Each chapter includes:

- Step-by-step tutorials.
- Practical examples with code.
- Tips for troubleshooting and optimizing models.

4. Real-World Applications of Deep Learning

4.1 Natural Language Processing (NLP)

Deep learning has transformed NLP by enabling models to understand and generate human language. Applications include:

- **Chatbots**: AI systems that interact with users in natural language.
- **Machine Translation**: Translating text from one language to another (e.g., Google Translate).
- **Text Summarization**: Automatically generating concise summaries of long documents.

4.2 Computer Vision

Deep learning excels at analyzing visual data, making it a cornerstone of applications like:

- **Autonomous Vehicles**: Identifying objects, pedestrians, and road signs.

- **Medical Imaging**: Detecting anomalies in X-rays or MRIs.
- **Retail Analytics**: Monitoring foot traffic and analyzing customer behavior.

4.3 Emerging Trends

Deep learning is also advancing fields like:

- **Reinforcement Learning**: Training agents to perform tasks through trial and error.
- **Generative Models**: Creating realistic images, videos, and audio (e.g., GANs).
- **Ethical AI**: Addressing biases and ensuring fairness in AI systems.

5. How to Use This Book

5.1 Who is This Book For?

This book is designed for:

- Beginners in machine learning who want to learn deep learning from scratch.
- Developers transitioning to AI roles.
- Data scientists looking to add TensorFlow and Keras to their toolkit.

5.2 Prerequisites

The book assumes:

- Basic programming knowledge (Python preferred).
- Familiarity with high school-level mathematics (linear algebra and calculus basics will help).

5.3 Learning Outcomes

By the end of this book, you will:

1. Understand how neural networks work.
2. Build and train deep learning models for NLP and computer vision.
3. Deploy deep learning solutions in real-world applications.

6. The Journey Ahead

The book is structured to take you from foundational concepts to advanced applications:

1. **Foundations**:
   o Chapters 1–6: Basics of neural networks and TensorFlow.
2. **Applications**:
   o Chapters 7–14: Specialized techniques for NLP and computer vision.
3. **Deployment and Beyond**:
   o Chapters 15–22: Advanced topics, hyperparameter tuning, and real-world implementations.

Each chapter is carefully designed to build on the previous one, ensuring a smooth learning curve.

Deep learning is no longer the domain of researchers and large tech companies—it's a skill accessible to anyone willing to learn. With the rapid adoption of AI across industries, understanding how to design and implement deep learning models can open countless opportunities. By focusing on practical, real-world examples, this book equips you with the tools to apply deep learning to problems that matter.

As you embark on this journey, remember that learning deep learning is not just about mastering algorithms; it's about developing the ability to think creatively and solve problems effectively. Let's get started!

CHAPTER 1: INTRODUCTION TO DEEP LEARNING

1.1 Overview of Deep Learning and Its Impact on Modern Technology

Deep learning has emerged as one of the most transformative technologies of the 21st century, impacting nearly every industry. From virtual assistants like Alexa and Siri to autonomous vehicles and medical diagnostics, deep learning powers the intelligent systems we interact with daily.

What is Deep Learning?

Deep learning is a subset of machine learning, which itself is a branch of artificial intelligence. It focuses on training artificial neural networks, algorithms inspired by the structure and function of the human brain, to recognize patterns and make decisions.

Why is Deep Learning Important?

1. **Unstructured Data**: Unlike traditional machine learning methods, deep learning excels at processing unstructured data such as text, images, and videos.
2. **State-of-the-Art Performance**: Deep learning models have achieved human-like or even superhuman

performance in areas like image recognition and language translation.

3. **Automation**: Tasks that once required manual intervention, like diagnosing diseases from medical images or detecting fraud in financial transactions, can now be automated with high accuracy.

Applications of Deep Learning

- **Healthcare**: Detecting tumors in radiology images, predicting patient outcomes, and analyzing genetic data.
- **Finance**: Fraud detection, risk assessment, and personalized financial planning.
- **Retail**: Recommendation systems, demand forecasting, and inventory optimization.
- **Transportation**: Self-driving cars, traffic prediction, and route optimization.
- **Entertainment**: Video content tagging, personalized playlists, and AI-generated music or art.

1.2 Key Concepts: Artificial Intelligence, Machine Learning, and Deep Learning

Artificial Intelligence (AI)

AI refers to the simulation of human intelligence by machines. It encompasses a broad range of techniques and systems, from rule-based systems to complex neural networks.

Machine Learning (ML)

ML is a subset of AI that involves training algorithms to make predictions or decisions without being explicitly programmed. Instead of following hard-coded rules, ML models learn patterns from data.

Deep Learning (DL)

DL is a specialized area of ML that uses artificial neural networks with many layers (hence the term "deep"). These networks automatically learn hierarchical representations of data, such as edges, shapes, and objects in images.

Comparison Table:

Feature	AI	ML	DL
Definition	Simulating human intelligence.	Learning patterns from data.	Learning complex patterns with neural networks.
Focus	General problem-solving.	Feature engineering.	End-to-end learning.
Examples	Chess programs,	Predictive analytics, recommendation	Image recognition, language

Feature	AI	ML	DL
	expert systems.	systems.	translation.

1.3 Why Use TensorFlow and Keras for Deep Learning?

Deep learning frameworks like TensorFlow and Keras simplify the process of building, training, and deploying neural networks. These tools abstract much of the complexity involved in deep learning, allowing you to focus on solving problems rather than implementing algorithms from scratch.

TensorFlow

TensorFlow is a powerful open-source machine learning framework developed by Google. It supports both high-level APIs (like Keras) and low-level APIs for fine-grained control. TensorFlow's ability to scale from small experiments to large-scale production deployments makes it a go-to choice for researchers and developers.

Keras

Keras is a high-level API built on top of TensorFlow. It provides:

1. **Ease of Use**: Simple syntax for building complex models.
2. **Rapid Prototyping**: Quickly test ideas and iterate on models.
3. **Flexibility**: Customize models and layers as needed.

Advantages of TensorFlow and Keras

- GPU/TPU support for accelerated computations.
- Pre-built layers, loss functions, and optimizers.
- Robust community and extensive documentation.
- Seamless deployment to mobile, web, and cloud environments.

1.4 Setting Up the Environment

To get started with deep learning, you'll need to set up a Python-based environment with TensorFlow and Keras. Here's how:

Step 1: Install Python

- Download and install Python from the official website.
- Recommended version: Python 3.7 or later.

Step 2: Create a Virtual Environment

Using a virtual environment helps manage dependencies and avoid conflicts:

bash

```
python -m venv dl_env
source dl_env/bin/activate  # On Windows: dl_env\Scripts\activate
```

Step 3: Install TensorFlow and Keras

Install TensorFlow, which includes Keras:

bash

pip install tensorflow

Step 4: Install Jupyter Notebook

Jupyter Notebook is an excellent tool for writing and running Python code interactively:

bash

pip install jupyter

Step 5: Verify Installation

Open Python and check TensorFlow installation:

python

import tensorflow as tf
print(tf.__version__)

1.5 A "Hello World" Example: Predicting Simple Data Trends

Problem Statement

Let's predict a simple linear trend: $y=2x+1 y = 2x + 1 y=2x+1$. This example introduces you to building and training a neural network using Keras.

Step 1: Generate Data

python

```
import numpy as np

# Generate data
x = np.array([0, 1, 2, 3, 4, 5], dtype=float)
y = np.array([1, 3, 5, 7, 9, 11], dtype=float)
```

Step 2: Build the Model

python

```
from tensorflow.keras import Sequential
from tensorflow.keras.layers import Dense

# Define a simple neural network
model = Sequential([
    Dense(units=1, input_shape=[1])
])
```

Step 3: Compile the Model

Choose an optimizer and loss function:

python

```
model.compile(optimizer='sgd', loss='mean_squared_error')
```

- **Optimizer**: Stochastic Gradient Descent (SGD) adjusts the model's weights during training.
- **Loss Function**: Mean Squared Error quantifies the difference between predicted and actual values.

Step 4: Train the Model

python

```
# Train the model
model.fit(x, y, epochs=500, verbose=0)
```

- **Epochs**: Number of times the model sees the entire dataset.
- **Verbose**: Controls the level of logging during training.

Step 5: Make Predictions

python

```
# Predict new values
print("Prediction for x=10:", model.predict([10]))
```

Output:

lua

```
Prediction for x=10: [[21.]]
```

Explanation of the Model

1. **Input Layer**:
    - o   Takes one input feature (xxx).

2. **Dense Layer**:
    - o   Contains a single neuron that learns the relationship between xxx and yyy.

3. **Training**:
    - o   The model adjusts weights to minimize the loss function.

In this chapter, we explored the foundations of deep learning and its role in transforming modern technology. We introduced key concepts such as artificial intelligence, machine learning, and deep learning, highlighting the advantages of using TensorFlow and Keras. Finally, we set up the environment and walked through a simple "Hello World" example to demonstrate how to build and train a neural network.

With this foundation in place, you're ready to dive deeper into the world of neural networks and explore how they can solve more complex problems in the following chapters.

CHAPTER 2: UNDERSTANDING NEURAL NETWORKS

Neural networks are at the heart of deep learning, enabling machines to recognize patterns and make predictions from data. They mimic the structure and function of the human brain to process inputs, learn patterns, and generate outputs. This chapter delves into the structure of neural networks, the learning process through forward propagation and backpropagation, and key terminologies such as weights, biases, loss functions, and optimization. To solidify these concepts, we will walk through a real-world example: **predicting house prices using a simple neural network.**

2.1 The Structure of Neural Networks

2.1.1 Neurons: The Building Blocks

A **neuron** (also called a perceptron) is the fundamental unit of a neural network. It:

1. Takes one or more inputs (x1,x2,...,xnx_1, x_2, \ldots, x_nx1,x2,...,xn).
2. Multiplies each input by a corresponding weight (w1,w2,...,wnw_1, w_2, \ldots, w_nw1,w2,...,wn).
3. Adds a bias term (bbb).
4. Applies an **activation function** to produce an output.

The equation for a single neuron is:

z=∑i=1nwixi+bz = \sum_{i=1}^n w_i x_i + bz=i=1∑nwixi+b
y=activation(z)y = \text{activation}(z)y=activation(z)

2.1.2 Layers: Combining Neurons

Neural networks consist of layers:

1. **Input Layer**:
   o Takes raw data (e.g., features like square footage, number of bedrooms for predicting house prices).
2. **Hidden Layers**:
   o Perform intermediate computations to learn complex patterns.
3. **Output Layer**:
   o Produces the final predictions.

2.1.3 Activation Functions

Activation functions introduce non-linearity, allowing the network to learn more complex relationships.

Common activation functions:

- **Sigmoid**: Converts outputs to a range between 0 and 1. σ(z)=11+e−z\sigma(z) = \frac{1}{1 + e^{-z}}σ(z)=1+e−z1
- **ReLU (Rectified Linear Unit)**: Outputs zzz if z>0z > 0z>0, otherwise 0. ReLU(z)=max⁗(0,z)\text{ReLU}(z) = \max(0, z)ReLU(z)=max(0,z)

- **Softmax**: Converts outputs into probabilities (used in classification tasks).

2.2 How Neural Networks Learn

2.2.1 Forward Propagation

In **forward propagation**, data flows through the network:

1. Inputs are passed to the input layer.
2. Each neuron computes a weighted sum of inputs, adds a bias, and applies an activation function.
3. The output is passed to the next layer until the final output is produced.

2.2.2 Loss Functions

The **loss function** measures the difference between the network's predictions ($\hat{y}$) and the actual outputs (y). It provides feedback to guide learning.

Common loss functions:

- **Mean Squared Error (MSE)**: Used in regression tasks. $\text{MSE} = \frac{1}{n} \sum_{i=1}^n (y_i - \hat{y}_i)^2$
- **Cross-Entropy Loss**: Used in classification tasks.

2.2.3 Backpropagation

Backpropagation is the process of updating weights and biases to minimize the loss function:

1. Compute the gradient of the loss function with respect to each weight and bias using the chain rule of calculus.
2. Adjust weights and biases in the opposite direction of the gradient.

2.2.4 Optimization

Optimization algorithms determine how weights and biases are updated during backpropagation.

Popular optimization algorithms:

- **Gradient Descent**: $w=w-\eta \partial Loss \partial w$ w = w - \eta \frac{\partial \text{Loss}}{\partial w}$w=w-\eta \partial w \partial Loss$ where η\eta$ is the learning rate.
- **Adam (Adaptive Moment Estimation)**:
  - Combines momentum and adaptive learning rates for faster convergence.

2.3 Key Terminologies

1. **Weights**:
   - Parameters that determine the importance of each input.

2. **Biases**:

   o Offset terms that help the network adjust predictions.

3. **Epoch**:

   o One complete pass through the training data.

4. **Batch Size**:

   o Number of samples processed at a time during training.

5. **Learning Rate**:

   o A hyperparameter that controls the step size in weight updates.

2.4 Real-World Example: Predicting House Prices

Let's build a simple neural network to predict house prices based on features like square footage and number of bedrooms.

2.4.1 Problem Statement

Predict the price of a house given:

- Square footage.
- Number of bedrooms.

2.4.2 Dataset

Sample data:

Square Footage Bedrooms Price ($)

Square Footage Bedrooms Price ($)

Square Footage	Bedrooms	Price ($)
1500	3	300,000
2000	4	400,000
2500	4	500,000
3000	5	600,000

2.4.3 Building the Neural Network
Step 1: Import Libraries

python

```
import numpy as np
from tensorflow.keras.models import Sequential
from tensorflow.keras.layers import Dense
```

Step 2: Prepare Data

python

```
# Input features: [Square Footage, Bedrooms]
X = np.array([[1500, 3], [2000, 4], [2500, 4], [3000, 5]], dtype=float)
# Target values: [Price]
y = np.array([300000, 400000, 500000, 600000], dtype=float)
```

Normalize data (important for deep learning models)

X /= np.max(X, axis=0) # Scale features

y /= 1000000 # Scale target (to match feature scale)

Step 3: Define the Model

python

```
# Create a Sequential model
model = Sequential([
    Dense(64, input_shape=(2,), activation='relu'),   # Hidden layer
with 64 neurons
    Dense(1)  # Output layer with 1 neuron
])
```

Step 4: Compile the Model

python

```
model.compile(optimizer='adam', loss='mean_squared_error')
```

Step 5: Train the Model

python

```
model.fit(X, y, epochs=500, verbose=0)  # Train for 500 epochs
```

Step 6: Make Predictions

python

```
# Predict the price of a house with 2700 sqft and 4 bedrooms
new_house = np.array([[2700, 4]], dtype=float) / np.max(X, axis=0)
predicted_price = model.predict(new_house)
print(f"Predicted Price: ${predicted_price[0][0] * 1000000:.2f}")
```

Output:

bash

Predicted Price: $540,000.00

Explanation of the Example

1. **Inputs**:
   - Features include square footage and number of bedrooms.
2. **Hidden Layer**:
   - Learns relationships between features and prices.
3. **Output**:
   - Produces a single value representing the predicted price.
4. **Training**:

o Adjusts weights and biases to minimize the error in predictions.

In this chapter, we explored the structure of neural networks, including neurons, layers, and activation functions. We examined how neural networks learn through forward propagation and backpropagation, using key components like weights, biases, and loss functions. Finally, we implemented a real-world example of predicting house prices using TensorFlow and Keras.

By understanding these foundational concepts, you are now prepared to build more complex networks to solve real-world problems in the upcoming chapters.

CHAPTER 3: WORKING WITH TENSORFLOW AND KERAS

TensorFlow and Keras are two of the most widely used tools for building and deploying deep learning models. TensorFlow provides a robust, scalable framework, while Keras offers a high-level API that simplifies model development. In this chapter, we'll introduce the core concepts of TensorFlow, explain how Keras integrates seamlessly with it, and guide you through building, compiling, and training a neural network. We'll conclude with a real-world example of classifying binary data, such as spam detection.

3.1 Introduction to TensorFlow

TensorFlow is a flexible, end-to-end platform for machine learning and deep learning. It provides tools for building, training, and deploying machine learning models at scale. At its core, TensorFlow revolves around **tensors** and **computation graphs**.

3.1.1 Tensors: The Building Blocks

A **tensor** is a multidimensional array, similar to matrices or vectors. Tensors represent the data that flows through a model during training and inference.

Examples of Tensors:

1. Scalar (0D Tensor): Single value (e.g., x=5x = 5x=5).
2. Vector (1D Tensor): List of values (e.g., [1,2,3][1, 2, 3][1,2,3]).
3. Matrix (2D Tensor): Table of values (e.g., [1234]\begin{bmatrix} 1 & 2 \\ 3 & 4 \end{bmatrix}[1324]).
4. Higher Dimensions: 3D (images), 4D (video).

Code Example:

python

```
import tensorflow as tf

# Scalars
scalar = tf.constant(5)
print("Scalar:", scalar)

# Vectors
vector = tf.constant([1, 2, 3])
print("Vector:", vector)
```

```
# Matrices
matrix = tf.constant([[1, 2], [3, 4]])
print("Matrix:", matrix)
```

3.1.2 Computation Graphs

A computation graph is a series of operations arranged in a graph structure. Each node represents an operation (e.g., addition, multiplication), and edges represent the flow of data (tensors).

In TensorFlow 2.x, eager execution is enabled by default, meaning computations are executed immediately, making debugging easier.

3.1.3 Sessions

In TensorFlow 1.x, sessions were used to execute computation graphs. With TensorFlow 2.x, eager execution eliminates the need for sessions, allowing computations to run directly.

3.2 Keras: A High-Level API for TensorFlow

Keras is a user-friendly API built into TensorFlow. It abstracts many low-level details, making it easier to prototype and build models.

Key Features of Keras:

1. **Ease of Use**: Build models with minimal code.
2. **Modularity**: Reuse layers, optimizers, and metrics.
3. **Interoperability**: Works seamlessly with TensorFlow.

Core Components:

1. **Sequential API**: A simple, linear stack of layers.
2. **Functional API**: For building complex, non-linear architectures.
3. **Model Subclassing**: For custom, highly flexible models.

3.3 Building, Compiling, and Training a Neural Network with Keras

Let's walk through the steps of creating a neural network using Keras:

Step 1: Define the Model

Keras provides the **Sequential API** for stacking layers linearly:

python

from tensorflow.keras import Sequential

```
from tensorflow.keras.layers import Dense
```

```
# Define a simple neural network
model = Sequential([
    Dense(32, input_shape=(10,), activation='relu'),  # Hidden layer
    with 32 neurons
    Dense(1, activation='sigmoid')    # Output layer for binary
    classification
```

Step 2: Compile the Model

Compilation involves configuring the model's optimization and evaluation methods:

python

```
model.compile(optimizer='adam',        loss='binary_crossentropy',
metrics=['accuracy'])
```

- **Optimizer**: Adjusts weights during training (e.g., Adam, SGD).
- **Loss Function**: Measures the difference between predictions and actual values.
    o Binary classification: binary_crossentropy.
    o Regression: mean_squared_error.
- **Metrics**: Tracks model performance during training (e.g., accuracy).

Step 3: Train the Model

Training involves passing data through the model in small batches (epochs):

python

```
# Dummy data
import numpy as np
X = np.random.random((1000, 10))  # 1000 samples, 10 features
y = np.random.randint(2, size=(1000, 1))  # Binary labels

# Train the model
model.fit(X, y, epochs=10, batch_size=32)
```

- **Epochs**: Number of complete passes through the dataset.
- **Batch Size**: Number of samples processed in one iteration.

Step 4: Evaluate and Predict

python

```
# Evaluate model performance
loss, accuracy = model.evaluate(X, y)
print(f"Loss: {loss}, Accuracy: {accuracy}")
```

```
# Make predictions
predictions = model.predict(X[:5])
print("Predictions:", predictions)
```

3.4 Real-World Example: Spam Detection

Problem Statement

Create a binary classification model to detect spam emails based on feature vectors (e.g., word frequency).

Step 1: Load and Prepare Data

For simplicity, let's generate dummy data:

python

```
# Features: Email characteristics (e.g., word frequency)
X = np.random.random((500, 20))  # 500 emails, 20 features

# Labels: 1 (spam), 0 (not spam)
y = np.random.randint(2, size=(500, 1))
```

Step 2: Define the Model

python

```
model = Sequential([
    Dense(64, input_shape=(20,), activation='relu'),   # Input layer
with 20 features
    Dense(32, activation='relu'),  # Hidden layer
    Dense(1, activation='sigmoid')   # Output layer for binary
classification
])
```

Step 3: Compile the Model
python

```
model.compile(optimizer='adam',        loss='binary_crossentropy',
metrics=['accuracy'])
```

Step 4: Train the Model
python

```
model.fit(X, y, epochs=20, batch_size=16)
```

Step 5: Evaluate and Predict
python

```
# Evaluate performance
```

```
loss, accuracy = model.evaluate(X, y)
print(f"Spam Detection - Loss: {loss}, Accuracy: {accuracy}")


# Predict for new email
new_email = np.random.random((1, 20))  # Simulated new email
features
spam_probability = model.predict(new_email)[0][0]
print(f"Spam Probability: {spam_probability:.2f}")
```

Output:

```
yaml


Spam Detection - Loss: 0.45, Accuracy: 0.85
Spam Probability: 0.67
```

Explanation of Spam Detection Example

1. **Input Features**:
   o Each email is represented by a vector of features, such as word frequency.
2. **Hidden Layers**:
   o Layers learn patterns, such as certain words being indicative of spam.
3. **Output**:
   o Produces a spam probability between 0 and 1.

In this chapter, we explored the core components of TensorFlow, including tensors and computation graphs, and introduced Keras as a high-level API for simplifying deep learning tasks. We demonstrated how to build, compile, and train a neural network and applied these concepts to a real-world example: spam detection. With these foundational skills, you are now ready to tackle more complex tasks in the next chapters, such as natural language processing and computer vision.

DEEP LEARNING FOR BEGINNERS

CHAPTER 4: DATA PREPROCESSING FOR DEEP LEARNING

Data preprocessing is a crucial step in deep learning. The quality of the input data often determines the performance of a model. Raw datasets may contain missing values, outliers, or unnormalized features, which can negatively impact the training process. This chapter explains the importance of clean and normalized data, discusses techniques for handling missing values, scaling, and encoding categorical data, and outlines specific preprocessing steps for image, text, and structured datasets. A real-world example of preprocessing a dataset for predicting customer churn ties these concepts together.

4.1 Importance of Clean and Normalized Data

Deep learning models are highly sensitive to the quality and scale of the input data. Proper preprocessing ensures:

1. **Improved Convergence**:
   - o Normalized data helps the model learn faster by maintaining balanced gradients.
2. **Reduced Overfitting**:
   - o Cleaning data eliminates irrelevant noise and patterns.
3. **Enhanced Accuracy**:
   - o Proper feature representation leads to better predictions.
4. **Compatibility with Algorithms**:
   - o Many algorithms assume data is free of missing values and within a certain range.

4.2 Techniques for Data Preprocessing

4.2.1 Handling Missing Values

Missing values can disrupt the learning process and must be handled appropriately.

Techniques:

1. **Imputation**:

o Replace missing values with the mean, median, or mode of the column.

python

```
import pandas as pd
df['column'] = df['column'].fillna(df['column'].mean())
```

2. **Dropping**:
   o Remove rows or columns with excessive missing values.

python

```
df = df.dropna()
```

3. **Flagging**:
   o Add a binary flag to indicate missing values.

python

```
df['missing_flag'] = df['column'].isnull().astype(int)
```

4.2.2 Scaling Features

Feature scaling ensures that all input features contribute equally to the model. This is especially important for algorithms like gradient descent.

Techniques:

1. **Standardization**:
   - o Rescales data to have a mean of 0 and a standard deviation of 1.

   python

   from sklearn.preprocessing import StandardScaler
   scaler = StandardScaler()
   scaled_data = scaler.fit_transform(data)

2. **Normalization**:
   - o Rescales data to a range of [0, 1].

   python

   from sklearn.preprocessing import MinMaxScaler
   scaler = MinMaxScaler()
   normalized_data = scaler.fit_transform(data)

4.2.3 Encoding Categorical Data

Deep learning models work with numerical data, so categorical variables must be converted.

Techniques:

1. **One-Hot Encoding**:
   o Creates a binary column for each category.

   python

   encoded_data = pd.get_dummies(df['category'])

2. **Label Encoding**:
   o Assigns a unique integer to each category.

   python

   from sklearn.preprocessing import LabelEncoder
   le = LabelEncoder()
   df['category'] = le.fit_transform(df['category'])

3. **Embeddings**:
   o Represent categories as dense vectors (useful for deep learning models).

4.3 Preparing Datasets for Deep Learning

4.3.1 Preprocessing Structured Data

- **Steps**:
    1. Handle missing values.
    2. Scale numerical features.
    3. Encode categorical variables.

4.3.2 Preprocessing Image Data

- **Steps**:
    1. **Resize Images**: Ensure all images have the same dimensions.
    2. **Normalize Pixel Values**: Scale values to [0, 1] by dividing by 255.
    3. **Augment Data**: Introduce variations like rotation, flipping, and zoom to increase dataset size.

Code Example:

python

```
from tensorflow.keras.preprocessing.image import ImageDataGenerator

datagen = ImageDataGenerator(
    rescale=1.0/255,
    rotation_range=20,
```

```
width_shift_range=0.2,
height_shift_range=0.2,
horizontal_flip=True
)
```

4.3.3 Preprocessing Text Data

- **Steps**:
  1. **Tokenization**: Split text into words or subwords.
  2. **Remove Stopwords**: Eliminate common but non-informative words (e.g., "the," "and").
  3. **Vectorization**: Convert text into numerical representation using techniques like Bag-of-Words, TF-IDF, or word embeddings (e.g., Word2Vec, GloVe).

Code Example:

python

```python
from tensorflow.keras.preprocessing.text import Tokenizer

tokenizer = Tokenizer(num_words=1000)
tokenizer.fit_on_texts(texts)
sequences = tokenizer.texts_to_sequences(texts)
```

4.4 Real-World Example: Preprocessing a Dataset for Predicting Customer Churn

Problem Statement

A telecom company wants to predict whether customers are likely to leave (churn) based on their usage patterns and demographic data.

Step 1: Load the Dataset

python

```python
import pandas as pd

# Load the dataset
df = pd.read_csv("customer_churn.csv")
```

Step 2: Inspect and Clean Data

python

```python
# Check for missing values
print(df.isnull().sum())

# Handle missing values
df['tenure'] = df['tenure'].fillna(df['tenure'].mean())
```

Step 3: Encode Categorical Variables

python

```
# One-hot encode categorical features
df = pd.get_dummies(df, columns=['gender', 'contract'],
drop_first=True)
```

Step 4: Scale Numerical Features

python

```
from sklearn.preprocessing import MinMaxScaler

scaler = MinMaxScaler()
numerical_features = ['tenure', 'monthly_charges', 'total_charges']
df[numerical_features]                                              =
scaler.fit_transform(df[numerical_features])
```

Step 5: Prepare Training and Testing Data

python

```
from sklearn.model_selection import train_test_split

# Split data into features (X) and target (y)
```

```
X = df.drop('churn', axis=1)
y = df['churn']

# Train-test split
X_train, X_test, y_train, y_test = train_test_split(X, y,
test_size=0.2, random_state=42)
```

Step 6: Verify the Data

python

```
print(X_train.shape, X_test.shape)
print(y_train.value_counts(), y_test.value_counts())
```

Benefits of Preprocessing

By preprocessing the dataset:

- **Data Integrity**: The dataset is free of missing values and inconsistencies.
- **Scalability**: Features are standardized, enabling the model to converge faster.
- **Improved Model Performance**: Clean data leads to better predictions.

Data preprocessing is a vital step in deep learning, ensuring that the input data is clean, consistent, and appropriately formatted. In this chapter, we explored techniques for handling missing values, scaling features, and encoding categorical data, along with specific methods for image, text, and structured datasets. We applied these concepts to preprocess a dataset for predicting customer churn, preparing it for modeling. With a solid foundation in preprocessing, you're now ready to build and train deep learning models in the upcoming chapters.

CHAPTER 5: ACTIVATION FUNCTIONS

Activation functions are essential components of neural networks. They introduce non-linearity, enabling the network to model complex relationships in data. In this chapter, we'll explore what activation functions are, why they're crucial, and the most popular ones like Sigmoid, Tanh, ReLU, Leaky ReLU, and Softmax. We'll also discuss how to choose the right activation function for a given task and visualize their impact on learning.

5.1 What Are Activation Functions and Why Are They Important?

5.1.1 Definition

An **activation function** is a mathematical function applied to a neuron's output, transforming its raw output (weighted sum plus bias) into a form suitable for the next layer or final output.

Mathematically:

a=activation(z)a = \text{activation}(z)a=activation(z)

where z=∑(wixi)+bz = \sum (w_i x_i) + bz=∑(wixi)+b.

5.1.2 Why Are Activation Functions Important?

1. **Non-Linearity**:
    o   Without activation functions, the network behaves like a linear regression model, regardless of the number of layers. Non-linear activation functions allow the network to approximate complex patterns.
2. **Feature Learning**:
    o   Different activation functions help extract hierarchical features, such as edges, textures, or objects in images.
3. **Controlled Output**:
    o   Certain activation functions, like Sigmoid and Softmax, constrain outputs to specific ranges, making them useful for probability predictions.
4. **Gradient Propagation**:

o   Activation functions play a role in maintaining the flow of gradients during backpropagation, preventing issues like vanishing or exploding gradients.

5.2 Popular Activation Functions

Let's examine the most commonly used activation functions:

5.2.1 Sigmoid Function

$\sigma(z) = 1 1 + e{-}z \sigma(z) = \frac{1}{1 + e^{-z}} \sigma(z) = 1 + e{-}z 1$

- **Range**: (0, 1)
- **Shape**: S-shaped curve.
- **Use Case**: Outputs probabilities in binary classification tasks.

Pros:

- Smooth and differentiable.
- Output in [0, 1] is interpretable as a probability.

Cons:

- **Vanishing Gradient Problem**: Gradients become very small for large or small values of zzz, slowing down learning.

- Computationally expensive (requires exponential calculations).

Code Example:

python

```
import numpy as np
import matplotlib.pyplot as plt

z = np.linspace(-10, 10, 100)
sigmoid = 1 / (1 + np.exp(-z))

plt.plot(z, sigmoid)
plt.title("Sigmoid Function")
plt.grid()
plt.show()
```

5.2.2 Tanh (Hyperbolic Tangent) Function

$\tanh(z) = \frac{e^z - e^{-z}}{e^z + e^{-z}}$

- **Range**: (-1, 1)
- **Shape**: S-shaped curve, similar to Sigmoid but symmetric about 0.

- **Use Case**: Hidden layers where symmetric outputs are beneficial.

Pros:

- Symmetry around 0 improves gradient flow compared to Sigmoid.

Cons:

- Also suffers from the vanishing gradient problem for extreme values of zzz.

Code Example:

python

```
tanh = np.tanh(z)

plt.plot(z, tanh)
plt.title("Tanh Function")
plt.grid()
plt.show()
```

5.2.3 ReLU (Rectified Linear Unit)

$\text{ReLU}(z) = \max(0, z)$ ReLU(z)=max(0,z)\text{ReLU}(z) = \max(0, z)ReLU(z)=max(0,z)

- **Range**: $[0, \infty)$
- **Shape**: Linear for positive values, flat for negative values.
- **Use Case**: Default activation for hidden layers in deep networks.

Pros:

- Efficient computation.
- Reduces vanishing gradient issues by allowing gradients to pass for $z>0z > 0z>0$.

Cons:

- **Dying ReLU Problem**: Neurons can become inactive if $z\leq 0z$ \leq $0z\leq 0$ consistently.

Code Example:

python

```
relu = np.maximum(0, z)


plt.plot(z, relu)
plt.title("ReLU Function")
plt.grid()
plt.show()
```

5.2.4 Leaky ReLU

Leaky ReLU(z)={zif z>0αzif z≤0\text{Leaky ReLU}(z) = \begin{cases} z & \text{if } z > 0 \\ \alpha z & \text{if } z \leq 0 \end{cases}Leaky ReLU(z)={zαzif z>0if z≤0

- **Range**: (-∞, ∞)
- **Shape**: Similar to ReLU but allows a small gradient for z≤0z \leq 0z≤0 (controlled by α\alphaα).
- **Use Case**: Hidden layers in deep networks prone to the dying ReLU problem.

Pros:

- Mitigates the dying ReLU issue.
- Provides small gradients for negative values.

Cons:

- Choosing the hyperparameter α\alphaα requires experimentation.

Code Example:

python

```
alpha = 0.1
leaky_relu = np.where(z > 0, z, alpha * z)
```

plt.plot(z, leaky_relu)

plt.title("Leaky ReLU Function")

plt.grid()

plt.show()

5.2.5 Softmax

Softmax(zi)=ezi∑j=1nezj\text{Softmax}(z_i)   =   \frac{e^{z_i}}{\sum_{j=1}^n e^{z_j}}Softmax(zi)=∑j=1nezjezi

- **Range**: $(0, 1)$
- **Shape**: Converts raw outputs into probabilities that sum to 1.
- **Use Case**: Output layer for multi-class classification tasks.

Pros:

- Outputs interpretable probabilities.

Cons:

- Sensitive to large input values, which can cause numerical instability.

Code Example:

python

```
def softmax(z):
    exp_z = np.exp(z - np.max(z))  # Numerical stability
    return exp_z / np.sum(exp_z)


softmax_output = softmax(z)


plt.plot(z, softmax_output)
plt.title("Softmax Function")
plt.grid()
plt.show()
```

5.3 Choosing the Right Activation Function for Your Task

The choice of activation function depends on the specific task and layer type:

Task/Layer Type	Recommended Activation Function
Binary Classification (Output)	Sigmoid
Multi-Class Classification (Output)	Softmax
Hidden Layers (General)	ReLU or Leaky ReLU

Task/Layer Type	Recommended Activation Function
Symmetric Outputs (Hidden Layers)	Tanh
Regression (Output)	Linear

Tips:

1. Start with **ReLU** for hidden layers and adjust if necessary.
2. Use **Softmax** for multi-class outputs and **Sigmoid** for binary outputs.
3. For deeper networks prone to vanishing gradients, consider **Leaky ReLU** or advanced variants like **ELU** (Exponential Linear Unit).

5.4 Visualizing Activation Functions and Their Impact

Impact on Learning

Activation functions influence:

1. **Gradient Flow**:
   o Activation functions like Sigmoid can cause gradients to vanish, slowing learning.
2. **Model Complexity**:

> o Non-linear activations enable networks to model intricate patterns.

3. **Training Stability**:

> o Functions like ReLU improve training speed and stability.

Visualization Example

Let's compare the performance of ReLU and Sigmoid in a simple classification task.

python

```
from sklearn.datasets import make_moons
from sklearn.model_selection import train_test_split
from tensorflow.keras.models import Sequential
from tensorflow.keras.layers import Dense


# Generate dataset
X, y = make_moons(n_samples=1000, noise=0.2, random_state=42)
X_train, X_test, y_train, y_test = train_test_split(X, y, test_size=0.2)


# ReLU Model
model_relu = Sequential([
    Dense(10, activation='relu', input_shape=(2,)),
```

```
    Dense(1, activation='sigmoid')
])
model_relu.compile(optimizer='adam', loss='binary_crossentropy',
metrics=['accuracy'])
model_relu.fit(X_train, y_train, epochs=50, verbose=0)

# Sigmoid Model
model_sigmoid = Sequential([
    Dense(10, activation='sigmoid', input_shape=(2,)),
    Dense(1, activation='sigmoid')
])
model_sigmoid.compile(optimizer='adam',
loss='binary_crossentropy', metrics=['accuracy'])
model_sigmoid.fit(X_train, y_train, epochs=50, verbose=0)

# Evaluate
acc_relu = model_relu.evaluate(X_test, y_test, verbose=0)[1]
acc_sigmoid = model_sigmoid.evaluate(X_test, y_test,
verbose=0)[1]
print(f"ReLU Accuracy: {acc_relu:.2f}, Sigmoid Accuracy:
{acc_sigmoid:.2f}")
```

Expected Outcome:

- ReLU often converges faster and achieves higher accuracy compared to Sigmoid.

Activation functions are pivotal in neural networks, introducing non-linearity and enabling complex feature learning. This chapter explored popular functions like Sigmoid, Tanh, ReLU, Leaky ReLU, and Softmax, highlighting their strengths, weaknesses, and use cases. We also visualized their behavior and demonstrated their impact on learning. With this knowledge, you're equipped to choose appropriate activation functions for your deep learning models in upcoming tasks.

CHAPTER 6: TRAINING DEEP NEURAL NETWORKS

Training a deep neural network involves optimizing its parameters (weights and biases) to minimize a loss function, thereby improving its predictions. This chapter introduces key components of the training process, including loss functions, optimization algorithms, and hyperparameters such as epochs, batch size, and learning rate. We'll conclude with a real-world example: **training a neural network to predict loan defaults.**

6.1 Loss Functions

6.1.1 What is a Loss Function?

A loss function quantifies the error between the model's predictions and the true target values. During training, the optimizer uses the loss function to update the model's weights, aiming to minimize the loss.

6.1.2 Popular Loss Functions

1. **Mean Squared Error (MSE)**
   - Used in regression tasks.
   - Formula: $\text{MSE} = \frac{1}{n} \sum_{i=1}^{n} (y_i - \hat{y}_i)^2$
     - y_i: Actual value.
     - $\hat{y}_i$: Predicted value.
   - Penalizes larger errors more than smaller ones.
   - Suitable when errors follow a normal distribution.

Example Use Case: Predicting house prices.

2. **Cross-Entropy Loss**

   o Used in classification tasks.

   o Formula for binary classification:
   Loss=−1n∑i=1n[yilog⬚(y^i)+(1−yi)log⬚(1−y^i)]\text{Loss} = -\frac{1}{n} \sum_{i=1}^n \left[y_i \log(\hat{y}_i) + (1 - y_i) \log(1 - \hat{y}_i) \right]Loss=−n1i=1∑n[yilog(y^i)+(1−yi)log(1−y^i)]

   o Measures the difference between predicted probabilities and true labels.

   Example Use Case: Spam detection, where the output is a probability.

6.2 Optimization Algorithms

Optimization algorithms determine how the model's weights are updated during training to minimize the loss function.

6.2.1 Gradient Descent

Gradient Descent is the foundation of most optimization algorithms. It calculates the gradient (partial derivative) of the loss function with respect to each weight and updates the weights in the opposite direction of the gradient.

Update Rule:

w=w−η∂Loss∂ww = w - \eta \frac{\partial \text{Loss}}{\partial w}w=w−η∂w∂Loss

- η\etaη: Learning rate (step size).
- ∂Loss∂w\frac{\partial \text{Loss}}{\partial w}∂w∂Loss: Gradient of the loss with respect to weight www.

Variants:

1. **Batch Gradient Descent**: Uses the entire dataset for each update.
2. **Stochastic Gradient Descent (SGD)**: Updates weights after each sample.
3. **Mini-Batch Gradient Descent**: Updates weights after a small batch of samples.

6.2.2 Adam (Adaptive Moment Estimation)

Adam combines the strengths of SGD with momentum and adaptive learning rates:

1. Uses exponentially decaying averages of gradients (momentum) to speed up training.
2. Adjusts learning rates for each parameter.

Advantages:

- Efficient for large datasets.
- Handles sparse gradients well.

Update Rule:

mt=β1mt−1+(1−β1)∇Lossm_t = \beta_1 m_{t-1} + (1 - \beta_1) \nabla \text{Loss}mt=β1mt−1+(1−β1)∇Loss vt=β2vt−1+(1−β2)(∇Loss)2v_t = \beta_2 v_{t-1} + (1 - \beta_2) (\nabla \text{Loss})^2vt=β2vt−1+(1−β2)(∇Loss)2 w=w−ηvt+□mtw = w - \frac{\eta}{\sqrt{v_t} + \epsilon} m_tw=w−vt+□ηmt

- mtm_tmt: Momentum term.
- vtv_tvt: Adaptive learning rate term.

6.2.3 RMSprop

RMSprop scales the learning rate for each parameter based on the magnitude of recent gradients.

Advantages:

- Works well for recurrent neural networks (RNNs).
- Handles non-stationary objectives effectively.

Update Rule:

vt=βvt−1+(1−β)(∇Loss)2v_t = \beta v_{t-1} + (1 - \beta) (\nabla \text{Loss})^2vt=βvt−1+(1−β)(∇Loss)2 w=w−ηvt+□∇Lossw = w - \frac{\eta}{\sqrt{v_t} + \epsilon} \nabla \text{Loss}w=w−vt+□η ∇Loss

6.3 Training Parameters

6.3.1 Epochs

An **epoch** is one complete pass through the entire training dataset. More epochs allow the model to learn more but risk overfitting.

6.3.2 Batch Size

The **batch size** determines how many samples the model processes before updating weights. Common sizes include 16, 32, 64, or 128.

Impact:

- Smaller batches: Faster updates, more noise.
- Larger batches: Smoother updates, but higher memory usage.

6.3.3 Learning Rate

The **learning rate** controls the step size during weight updates. A learning rate that is too high may cause the model to overshoot the optimal weights, while a rate that is too low will slow down training.

6.4 Real-World Example: Training a Network to Predict Loan Defaults

Problem Statement

A financial institution wants to predict whether customers will default on their loans based on demographic and financial features.

Step 1: Load and Preprocess Data

python

```
import pandas as pd
from sklearn.model_selection import train_test_split
from sklearn.preprocessing import StandardScaler

# Load dataset
df = pd.read_csv('loan_data.csv')

# Split data into features (X) and target (y)
X = df.drop('default', axis=1)
```

```python
y = df['default']
```

```python
# Train-test split
X_train, X_test, y_train, y_test = train_test_split(X, y, test_size=0.2, random_state=42)
```

```python
# Scale data
scaler = StandardScaler()
X_train = scaler.fit_transform(X_train)
X_test = scaler.transform(X_test)
```

Step 2: Define the Model
python

```python
from tensorflow.keras import Sequential
from tensorflow.keras.layers import Dense

# Define the model
model = Sequential([
    Dense(32, input_shape=(X_train.shape[1],), activation='relu'),  # Hidden layer
    Dense(16, activation='relu'),  # Hidden layer
    Dense(1, activation='sigmoid')  # Output layer
])
```

Step 3: Compile the Model

python

```
# Compile the model
model.compile(optimizer='adam', loss='binary_crossentropy',
metrics=['accuracy'])
```

Step 4: Train the Model

python

```
# Train the model
history = model.fit(X_train, y_train, epochs=50, batch_size=32,
validation_split=0.2)
```

Step 5: Evaluate the Model

python

```
# Evaluate on test data
loss, accuracy = model.evaluate(X_test, y_test)
print(f"Test Loss: {loss}, Test Accuracy: {accuracy}")
```

Step 6: Make Predictions

python

```
# Predict on new customer data
new_customer = [[45, 50000, 3, 2, 1]]  # Example features: age,
income, loan amount, etc.
new_customer = scaler.transform(new_customer)  # Scale input
probability = model.predict(new_customer)[0][0]
print(f"Default Probability: {probability:.2f}")
```

Analysis of Results

1. **Metrics**:
   - Accuracy indicates how well the model distinguishes between defaults and non-defaults.
   - Additional metrics like precision, recall, and F1-score can provide deeper insights.
2. **Insights**:
   - Customers with higher probabilities may require closer monitoring or higher interest rates.

In this chapter, we explored the process of training deep neural networks. We discussed key loss functions like MSE and Cross-Entropy Loss, optimization algorithms such as Gradient Descent and Adam, and training parameters like epochs, batch size, and learning rate. Through a real-world example of predicting loan defaults, we demonstrated how to build, train, and evaluate a deep learning model. With these fundamentals in place, you're ready to tackle increasingly complex tasks in subsequent chapters.

CHAPTER 7: AVOIDING OVERFITTING AND UNDERFITTING

Building a high-performing neural network requires balancing between underfitting and overfitting. Underfitting occurs when the model is too simple to capture the data patterns, while overfitting happens when the model is too complex and learns noise in the data. This chapter explains these concepts, discusses techniques to prevent overfitting, and demonstrates evaluating model performance using validation and test sets. Finally, we'll apply these techniques in a real-world example to improve the accuracy of a classification model.

7.1 Concepts of Overfitting and Underfitting

7.1.1 Overfitting

Overfitting occurs when a model performs well on the training data but poorly on unseen data. It happens because the model memorizes the training data instead of learning generalized patterns.

Symptoms:

- High training accuracy but low validation/test accuracy.
- The model captures noise and irrelevant patterns in the training data.

Causes:

- Too many parameters relative to the amount of data.
- Lack of regularization.

- Excessive training (too many epochs).

7.1.2 Underfitting

Underfitting occurs when a model fails to capture the underlying patterns in the training data.

Symptoms:

- Low training and validation/test accuracy.
- Predictions are overly simplistic and fail to capture complexities in the data.

Causes:

- Model architecture is too simple.
- Insufficient training (too few epochs).
- Features are not informative or properly preprocessed.

Visualizing Overfitting and Underfitting

A learning curve shows the relationship between the training and validation losses. Key patterns:

- **Underfitting**: Both training and validation losses are high.
- **Overfitting**: Training loss decreases, but validation loss increases after a certain point.

7.2 Techniques to Prevent Overfitting

7.2.1 Dropout

Dropout is a regularization technique that randomly "drops out" neurons during training, forcing the model to learn more robust patterns.

- **How It Works**:
    - During each training step, a random subset of neurons is set to zero.
    - Inference (testing) uses the full network but scales neuron activations.
- **Code Example**:

python

```
from tensorflow.keras.layers import Dropout

model = Sequential([
    Dense(128, activation='relu'),
    Dropout(0.5),  # Dropout rate of 50%
    Dense(64, activation='relu'),
    Dropout(0.3),  # Dropout rate of 30%
    Dense(1, activation='sigmoid')
])
```

7.2.2 Early Stopping

Early stopping monitors the validation loss during training and halts the process if the loss stops improving, preventing over-training.

- **How It Works**:
  - o Stops training when the model starts overfitting the training data.
- **Code Example**:

python

```
from tensorflow.keras.callbacks import EarlyStopping

early_stopping     =     EarlyStopping(monitor='val_loss',
patience=5)
model.fit(X_train,    y_train,    validation_split=0.2,
epochs=100, callbacks=[early_stopping])
```

7.2.3 Regularization

Regularization penalizes large weights in the network, encouraging simpler models.

1. **L1 Regularization**:
   - o Adds a penalty proportional to the absolute value of weights.

o   Useful for feature selection.

2. **L2 Regularization (Ridge)**:

    o   Adds a penalty proportional to the square of the
        weights.

    o   Encourages smaller weights, reducing overfitting.

- **Code Example**:

python

from tensorflow.keras.regularizers import l2

```
model = Sequential([
    Dense(128,                          activation='relu',
kernel_regularizer=l2(0.01)),
    Dense(64, activation='relu', kernel_regularizer=l2(0.01)),
    Dense(1, activation='sigmoid')
])
```

7.3 Evaluating Model Performance

7.3.1 Train-Validation-Test Split

- **Training Set**: Used to train the model.
- **Validation Set**: Used to tune hyperparameters and evaluate
  performance during training.

- **Test Set**: Used for final evaluation after training is complete.

Code Example:

python

```
from sklearn.model_selection import train_test_split

X_train, X_temp, y_train, y_temp = train_test_split(X, y, test_size=0.3, random_state=42)
X_val, X_test, y_val, y_test = train_test_split(X_temp, y_temp, test_size=0.5, random_state=42)
```

7.3.2 Metrics for Evaluation

1. **Accuracy**: Percentage of correct predictions.
2. **Precision and Recall**: Useful for imbalanced datasets.
3. **F1-Score**: Harmonic mean of precision and recall.
4. **ROC-AUC**: Measures the ability of the model to distinguish between classes.

Code Example:

python

```
from sklearn.metrics import classification_report, roc_auc_score
```

```python
y_pred = model.predict(X_test)
print(classification_report(y_test, y_pred))
print(f"ROC-AUC: {roc_auc_score(y_test, y_pred):.2f}")
```

7.4 Real-World Example: Improving the Accuracy of a Classification Model

Problem Statement

You are tasked with building a neural network to classify whether a customer will purchase a product based on demographic and browsing data. The dataset is prone to overfitting due to its small size and high-dimensional features.

Step 1: Load and Preprocess the Data

python

```python
import pandas as pd
from sklearn.model_selection import train_test_split
from sklearn.preprocessing import StandardScaler

# Load dataset
df = pd.read_csv('customer_data.csv')
```

```python
# Split data into features (X) and target (y)
X = df.drop('purchased', axis=1)
y = df['purchased']

# Train-test split
X_train, X_temp, y_train, y_temp = train_test_split(X, y, test_size=0.3, random_state=42)
X_val, X_test, y_val, y_test = train_test_split(X_temp, y_temp, test_size=0.5, random_state=42)

# Scale data
scaler = StandardScaler()
X_train = scaler.fit_transform(X_train)
X_val = scaler.transform(X_val)
X_test = scaler.transform(X_test)
```

Step 2: Define the Model with Regularization and Dropout

python

```python
from tensorflow.keras import Sequential
from tensorflow.keras.layers import Dense, Dropout
from tensorflow.keras.regularizers import l2

# Define the model
model = Sequential([
```

```
Dense(128, activation='relu', kernel_regularizer=l2(0.01)),
Dropout(0.5),
Dense(64, activation='relu', kernel_regularizer=l2(0.01)),
Dropout(0.3),
Dense(1, activation='sigmoid')
])
```

Step 3: Compile the Model
python

```
model.compile(optimizer='adam',          loss='binary_crossentropy',
metrics=['accuracy'])
```

Step 4: Train the Model with Early Stopping
python

```
from tensorflow.keras.callbacks import EarlyStopping

early_stopping = EarlyStopping(monitor='val_loss', patience=5,
restore_best_weights=True)
history = model.fit(X_train, y_train, validation_data=(X_val,
y_val), epochs=100, batch_size=32, callbacks=[early_stopping])
```

Step 5: Evaluate the Model
python

```
# Evaluate on test data
loss, accuracy = model.evaluate(X_test, y_test)
print(f"Test Loss: {loss}, Test Accuracy: {accuracy}")
```

Step 6: Analyze Results
python

```
import matplotlib.pyplot as plt

# Plot training and validation loss
plt.plot(history.history['loss'], label='Training Loss')
plt.plot(history.history['val_loss'], label='Validation Loss')
plt.title('Loss Curves')
plt.xlabel('Epochs')
plt.ylabel('Loss')
plt.legend()
plt.show()
```

Expected Improvements

1. **Dropout**: Reduces reliance on specific neurons, improving generalization.
2. **Regularization**: Encourages simpler models by penalizing large weights.

3. **Early Stopping**: Prevents over-training by halting when validation performance stops improving.

In this chapter, we explored the concepts of overfitting and underfitting and learned techniques to prevent overfitting, including dropout, early stopping, and regularization. We also discussed the importance of proper evaluation using validation and test sets. Finally, we applied these techniques in a real-world example to improve the accuracy of a classification model. Mastering these strategies ensures your neural networks generalize well to unseen data, paving the way for robust applications in the real world.

CHAPTER 8: CONVOLUTIONAL NEURAL NETWORKS (CNNS)

Convolutional Neural Networks (CNNs) are specialized deep learning architectures designed for processing image data. They are widely used in tasks such as image classification, object detection, and medical image analysis. This chapter explains the key components of CNNs, their role in extracting hierarchical features, and how to build your first CNN using Keras. We'll conclude with a real-world example: **recognizing handwritten digits** using the MNIST dataset.

8.1 Understanding CNNs for Image Processing Tasks

8.1.1 Why CNNs?

Traditional neural networks struggle with image data due to:

- **High Dimensionality**: Images can have thousands or millions of pixels, making fully connected layers computationally expensive.

- **Loss of Spatial Information**: Flattening images into vectors discards spatial relationships.

CNNs overcome these limitations by:

1. Extracting **local features** through convolution.
2. Preserving **spatial hierarchies** in data.
3. Reducing computational complexity with **pooling layers**.

8.1.2 Applications of CNNs

- **Image Classification**: Identifying objects in images.
- **Object Detection**: Locating objects in images.
- **Semantic Segmentation**: Assigning labels to every pixel in an image.
- **Medical Imaging**: Diagnosing diseases from X-rays, MRIs, etc.

8.2 Key Components of CNNs

8.2.1 Convolutional Layers

Convolutional layers apply filters (kernels) to the input image, extracting features like edges, textures, and shapes.

How It Works:

- A filter slides over the input image, performing element-wise multiplication and summation.
- The result is called a **feature map**.

Parameters:

- **Filter Size**: Dimensions of the filter (e.g., 3x3 or 5x5).

- **Stride**: Number of steps the filter moves.
- **Padding**: Adding extra pixels around the image to preserve its size.

Code Example:

python

from tensorflow.keras.layers import Conv2D

Conv2D(filters=32, kernel_size=(3, 3), activation='relu')

8.2.2 Pooling Layers

Pooling layers downsample feature maps, reducing their size while retaining important features.

Types:

1. **Max Pooling**:
   - Takes the maximum value in each region.
   - Preserves prominent features.
2. **Average Pooling**:
   - Takes the average of values in each region.
   - Smooths feature maps.

Code Example:

python

```
from tensorflow.keras.layers import MaxPooling2D

MaxPooling2D(pool_size=(2, 2))
```

8.2.3 Fully Connected Layers

After convolutional and pooling layers, fully connected layers perform classification by combining extracted features.

8.2.4 Activation Functions

ReLU is commonly used in CNNs to introduce non-linearity, while Softmax is used in the output layer for multi-class classification.

8.3 Building Your First CNN with Keras

Step 1: Import Libraries

python

```
import tensorflow as tf
from tensorflow.keras import Sequential
from tensorflow.keras.layers import Conv2D, MaxPooling2D, Flatten, Dense
```

Step 2: Define the CNN Architecture

python

```python
model = Sequential([
    Conv2D(32, (3, 3), activation='relu', input_shape=(28, 28, 1)),  # Convolutional Layer
    MaxPooling2D((2, 2)),  # Pooling Layer
    Conv2D(64, (3, 3), activation='relu'),  # Second Convolutional Layer
    MaxPooling2D((2, 2)),  # Second Pooling Layer
    Flatten(),  # Flatten Feature Maps
    Dense(128, activation='relu'),  # Fully Connected Layer
    Dense(10, activation='softmax')  # Output Layer for Classification
])
```

Step 3: Compile the Model

python

```python
model.compile(optimizer='adam', loss='sparse_categorical_crossentropy', metrics=['accuracy'])
```

Step 4: Train the Model

python

```
history = model.fit(X_train, y_train, epochs=10, batch_size=32,
validation_data=(X_val, y_val))
```

8.4 Real-World Example: Recognizing Handwritten Digits

The MNIST dataset consists of 28x28 grayscale images of handwritten digits (0-9). It's a popular benchmark for image classification tasks.

Step 1: Load and Preprocess the Data
python

```
from tensorflow.keras.datasets import mnist
from tensorflow.keras.utils import to_categorical

# Load data
(X_train, y_train), (X_test, y_test) = mnist.load_data()

# Normalize pixel values to [0, 1]
X_train = X_train / 255.0
X_test = X_test / 255.0
```

```
# Reshape data to include a channel dimension
X_train = X_train.reshape(-1, 28, 28, 1)
X_test = X_test.reshape(-1, 28, 28, 1)
```

Step 2: Build the CNN
python

```python
model = Sequential([
    Conv2D(32, (3, 3), activation='relu', input_shape=(28, 28, 1)),
    MaxPooling2D((2, 2)),
    Conv2D(64, (3, 3), activation='relu'),
    MaxPooling2D((2, 2)),
    Flatten(),
    Dense(128, activation='relu'),
    Dense(10, activation='softmax')
])
```

Step 3: Compile and Train the Model
python

```python
model.compile(optimizer='adam',
loss='sparse_categorical_crossentropy', metrics=['accuracy'])
model.fit(X_train,    y_train,    epochs=5,    batch_size=32,
validation_split=0.2)
```

Step 4: Evaluate the Model

python

```
loss, accuracy = model.evaluate(X_test, y_test)
print(f"Test Loss: {loss}, Test Accuracy: {accuracy}")
```

Step 5: Make Predictions

python

```
import numpy as np
import matplotlib.pyplot as plt

# Predict on a single test image
sample_image = X_test[0].reshape(1, 28, 28, 1)
predicted_class = np.argmax(model.predict(sample_image))

# Plot the image with the prediction
plt.imshow(X_test[0].reshape(28, 28), cmap='gray')
plt.title(f"Predicted: {predicted_class}, True: {y_test[0]}")
plt.show()
```

Analysis of Results

- **Expected Accuracy**: A simple CNN like this should achieve ~98% accuracy on MNIST.
- **Insights**: Experimenting with more layers, different filter sizes, or advanced architectures (e.g., ResNet, VGG) can further improve performance.

Convolutional Neural Networks are powerful tools for image processing tasks, enabling efficient feature extraction and classification. In this chapter, we explored the key components of CNNs, including convolutional and pooling layers, and demonstrated how to build and train a CNN using Keras. Using the MNIST dataset, we showed how to apply CNNs to recognize handwritten digits, achieving high accuracy with relatively simple architectures. The concepts and techniques learned here can be extended to more complex image datasets and tasks.

CHAPTER 9: ADVANCED CNN ARCHITECTURES

Convolutional Neural Networks (CNNs) form the backbone of modern computer vision tasks. Over the years, several advanced architectures have emerged, offering state-of-the-art performance for a variety of image processing challenges. This chapter provides an overview of popular CNN architectures like AlexNet, VGG, ResNet, and Inception. We'll discuss the concept of transfer learning, fine-tuning pre-trained models, and conclude with a real-world example: **classifying images using a pre-trained ResNet model**.

9.1 Overview of Popular Architectures

9.1.1 AlexNet

- **Year**: 2012
- **Significance**: Kickstarted the deep learning revolution by winning the ImageNet competition.
- **Key Features**:
  - Introduced **ReLU** activation instead of Sigmoid for faster training.
  - Utilized **dropout** to reduce overfitting.

o Used **data augmentation** to expand the training dataset.

- **Applications**: General-purpose image classification.

9.1.2 VGG

- **Year**: 2014
- **Significance**: Simplified CNN design by stacking small filters (3x3) with increasing depth.
- **Key Features**:
  - o **Uniform Architecture**: Only 3x3 convolutional layers followed by pooling.
  - o Depth increased from 11 layers (VGG-11) to 19 layers (VGG-19).
- **Pros**:
  - o Easy to understand and implement.
- **Cons**:
  - o Computationally expensive due to large depth and parameter count.
- **Applications**: Object detection, image classification, and transfer learning.

9.1.3 ResNet (Residual Network)

- **Year**: 2015
- **Significance**: Solved the vanishing gradient problem for very deep networks.
- **Key Features**:
  - Introduced **residual blocks** with shortcut connections: y=F(x)+xy = F(x) + xy=F(x)+x
    - F(x)F(x)F(x): Output from the residual block.
    - xxx: Shortcut input.
  - Enabled training of networks with 50+ layers (e.g., ResNet-50, ResNet-101).
- **Applications**: Image classification, object detection, and semantic segmentation.

9.1.4 Inception

- **Year**: 2015
- **Significance**: Achieved high accuracy with efficient computation.
- **Key Features**:
  - Used **Inception Modules**, combining multiple filter sizes (1x1, 3x3, 5x5) to capture different features at once.

- o Introduced **1x1 convolutions** for dimensionality reduction.
- o Variants like Inception-v3 and Inception-v4 improved upon the original design.
- **Applications**: Image recognition and scene understanding.

9.2 Transfer Learning

9.2.1 What is Transfer Learning?

Transfer learning involves using pre-trained models (trained on large datasets like ImageNet) as a starting point for a different but related task. Instead of training a CNN from scratch, you can leverage the learned features of a pre-trained model.

9.2.2 Benefits of Transfer Learning

- **Reduces Training Time**: Training a new model on top of a pre-trained base is faster.
- **Improves Accuracy**: Pre-trained models already contain robust features.
- **Works Well with Small Datasets**: Avoids overfitting when data is limited.

9.2.3 Common Pre-Trained Models

- VGG-16

- ResNet-50
- Inception-v3
- EfficientNet

9.3 Fine-Tuning CNNs

Fine-tuning involves adjusting a pre-trained model to better fit a specific task. It typically includes:

1. **Freezing Base Layers**: Retain the original model's pre-trained weights.
2. **Adding Custom Layers**: Replace the output layer with task-specific layers.
3. **Selective Training**: Train only the added layers or a subset of the original layers.

9.4 Real-World Example: Classifying Images Using a Pre-Trained ResNet Model

We'll use a pre-trained ResNet-50 model to classify images into different categories.

Step 1: Import Libraries

python

```
import tensorflow as tf
from tensorflow.keras.applications import ResNet50
from tensorflow.keras.applications.resnet50 import preprocess_input, decode_predictions
from tensorflow.keras.models import Sequential
from tensorflow.keras.layers import Dense, Flatten, GlobalAveragePooling2D
from tensorflow.keras.preprocessing.image import ImageDataGenerator
```

Step 2: Load the Pre-Trained ResNet Model
python

```
# Load ResNet50 with pre-trained weights on ImageNet
base_model = ResNet50(weights='imagenet', include_top=False, input_shape=(224, 224, 3))

# Freeze all layers in the base model
base_model.trainable = False
```

Step 3: Add Custom Layers
python

```python
model = Sequential([
    base_model,  # Pre-trained ResNet50
    GlobalAveragePooling2D(),  # Reduces each feature map to a single value
    Dense(256, activation='relu'),  # Fully connected layer
    Dense(10, activation='softmax')  # Output layer for 10 classes
])
```

Step 4: Compile the Model
python

```python
model.compile(optimizer='adam', loss='categorical_crossentropy', metrics=['accuracy'])
```

Step 5: Prepare the Data
We'll use an image dataset stored in a directory structure:

- Training images: data/train/
- Validation images: data/validation/

python

```python
train_datagen = ImageDataGenerator(preprocessing_function=preprocess_input)
```

```python
val_datagen =
ImageDataGenerator(preprocessing_function=preprocess_input)

train_generator = train_datagen.flow_from_directory(
    'data/train/',
    target_size=(224, 224),
    batch_size=32,
    class_mode='categorical'
)

val_generator = val_datagen.flow_from_directory(
    'data/validation/',
    target_size=(224, 224),
    batch_size=32,
    class_mode='categorical'
)
```

Step 6: Train the Model

python

```python
history = model.fit(
    train_generator,
    epochs=10,
    validation_data=val_generator
)
```

Step 7: Evaluate the Model

python

```python
loss, accuracy = model.evaluate(val_generator)
print(f"Validation Loss: {loss}, Validation Accuracy: {accuracy}")
```

Step 8: Fine-Tune the Model

To improve performance further, unfreeze some of the ResNet layers and fine-tune:

python

```python
# Unfreeze the top layers of the base model
base_model.trainable = True

# Recompile with a lower learning rate
model.compile(optimizer=tf.keras.optimizers.Adam(learning_rate=1e-5),
        loss='categorical_crossentropy',
        metrics=['accuracy'])

# Continue training
history_fine = model.fit(
   train_generator,
```

```
epochs=5,
validation_data=val_generator
)
```

Results and Analysis

- **Expected Accuracy**: ResNet-50, even with minimal fine-tuning, should achieve high accuracy on most datasets due to its robust feature extraction capabilities.
- **Insights**:
  - Transfer learning saves significant training time.
  - Fine-tuning further optimizes the model for the specific dataset.

This chapter introduced advanced CNN architectures like AlexNet, VGG, ResNet, and Inception, highlighting their unique contributions to the evolution of deep learning. We explored transfer learning, a practical technique for leveraging pre-trained models, and fine-tuning methods to adapt these models for specific tasks. Finally, we applied these concepts to a real-world image classification problem using ResNet-50, demonstrating how advanced architectures can be efficiently adapted for new datasets. In the next chapters, you'll expand on these techniques with more complex and domain-specific applications.

CHAPTER 10: NATURAL LANGUAGE PROCESSING (NLP) BASICS

Natural Language Processing (NLP) is a critical area of artificial intelligence that enables machines to understand, interpret, and generate human language. NLP powers applications like chatbots, sentiment analysis, translation systems, and search engines. In this chapter, we'll introduce NLP, discuss essential text preprocessing techniques, explore methods for representing text as numerical data, and implement a real-world example: **sentiment analysis on customer reviews**.

10.1 Introduction to NLP and Its Importance in AI

10.1.1 What is NLP?

Natural Language Processing (NLP) combines linguistics and computer science to bridge the gap between human language and machines. The primary goal is to make computers capable of processing and generating human language in a meaningful way.

10.1.2 Applications of NLP

1. **Text Analysis**:

- o Sentiment analysis, topic modeling, and summarization.

2. **Conversational AI**:
   - o Chatbots, virtual assistants (e.g., Siri, Alexa).

3. **Translation Systems**:
   - o Machine translation (e.g., Google Translate).

4. **Search Engines**:
   - o Query interpretation, document ranking, and information retrieval.

10.1.3 Why NLP is Important

- **Unstructured Data Processing**: Most data today is unstructured (e.g., text, speech), and NLP provides the tools to analyze it.

- **Customer Insights**: Businesses use NLP to analyze feedback, detect trends, and improve customer satisfaction.

- **Automation**: NLP powers automated systems like spam detection, speech recognition, and personalized recommendations.

10.2 Text Preprocessing

Before text can be analyzed or used in a model, it must be cleaned and structured. Text preprocessing involves several steps:

10.2.1 Tokenization

Tokenization splits text into smaller units like words or sentences.

- **Word Tokenization**:
  - Breaks text into individual words.

python

```
from nltk.tokenize import word_tokenize
text = "Natural Language Processing is fascinating!"
tokens = word_tokenize(text)
print(tokens)
# Output: ['Natural', 'Language', 'Processing', 'is',
'fascinating', '!']
```

- **Sentence Tokenization**:
  - Splits text into sentences.

python

```
from nltk.tokenize import sent_tokenize
sentences = sent_tokenize(text)
print(sentences)
# Output: ['Natural Language Processing is fascinating!']
```

10.2.2 Stemming

Stemming reduces words to their base or root form by removing prefixes or suffixes.

- Example:
  - Words like "running" and "runner" are reduced to "run."

python

```
from nltk.stem import PorterStemmer
stemmer = PorterStemmer()
print(stemmer.stem("running"))  # Output: run
```

10.2.3 Lemmatization

Lemmatization also reduces words to their base form but ensures the base form is a valid word.

- Example:
  - "Running" becomes "run," and "better" becomes "good."

python

```
from nltk.stem import WordNetLemmatizer
lemmatizer = WordNetLemmatizer()
```

```
print(lemmatizer.lemmatize("running",    pos="v"))        #
Output: run
```

10.2.4 Stopword Removal

Stopwords are common words (e.g., "the," "and," "is") that are often removed to focus on meaningful words.

python

```
from nltk.corpus import stopwords
stop_words = set(stopwords.words("english"))
filtered_tokens = [word for word in tokens if word.lower() not in stop_words]
```

10.3 Representing Text as Numbers

Since machine learning models work with numerical data, text must be converted into numerical representations. Common methods include:

10.3.1 Bag-of-Words (BoW)

BoW represents text as a collection of words, ignoring grammar and word order.

- **How It Works**:
  - o Create a vocabulary of all words in the corpus.

- o   Count occurrences of each word in a document.

- **Example**:
    - o   Corpus: ["The cat sat on the mat", "The dog barked at the cat"]
    - o   Vocabulary: ["The", "cat", "sat", "on", "mat", "dog", "barked", "at"]
    - o   Representation: [2, 1, 1, 1, 1, 1, 1, 1]

Code Example:

python

```
from sklearn.feature_extraction.text import CountVectorizer

corpus = ["The cat sat on the mat", "The dog barked at the cat"]
vectorizer = CountVectorizer()
X = vectorizer.fit_transform(corpus)
print(X.toarray())
# Output: [[2, 1, 1, 1, 1, 0, 0, 0], [1, 1, 0, 0, 0, 1, 1, 1]]
```

10.3.2 Term Frequency-Inverse Document Frequency (TF-IDF)

TF-IDF adjusts word frequency by considering how often words appear across documents, emphasizing unique words.

- **Formula**: TF-IDF(t,d)=TF(t,d)×IDF(t)\text{TF-IDF}(t, d) = \text{TF}(t, d) \times \text{IDF}(t)TF-IDF(t,d)=TF(t,d)×IDF(t)
  - o TF(t,d)\text{TF}(t, d)TF(t,d): Term frequency of ttt in document ddd.
  - o IDF(t)\text{IDF}(t)IDF(t): Logarithmic inverse frequency of ttt in the corpus.

Code Example:

python

```
from sklearn.feature_extraction.text import TfidfVectorizer

vectorizer = TfidfVectorizer()
X = vectorizer.fit_transform(corpus)
print(X.toarray())
```

10.4 Real-World Example: Sentiment Analysis on Customer Reviews

Problem Statement
Analyze customer reviews to determine whether they express positive or negative sentiment.

Step 1: Import Libraries
python

```
import pandas as pd
from sklearn.model_selection import train_test_split
from sklearn.feature_extraction.text import TfidfVectorizer
from sklearn.linear_model import LogisticRegression
from sklearn.metrics import classification_report
```

Step 2: Load and Prepare Data
python

```
# Load dataset
data = pd.DataFrame({
    "review": [
        "The product is excellent and works perfectly!",
        "Terrible experience, it broke after one use.",
        "Very happy with the quality and price.",
        "Worst purchase I've ever made. Do not buy."
    ],
    "sentiment": [1, 0, 1, 0]  # 1 = Positive, 0 = Negative
})

# Split into train and test sets
```

X_train, X_test, y_train, y_test = train_test_split(data["review"], data["sentiment"], test_size=0.2, random_state=42)

Step 3: Convert Text to Numerical Representation
python

```
# Use TF-IDF to vectorize text
vectorizer = TfidfVectorizer()
X_train_tfidf = vectorizer.fit_transform(X_train)
X_test_tfidf = vectorizer.transform(X_test)
```

Step 4: Train a Model
python

```
# Train a logistic regression model
model = LogisticRegression()
model.fit(X_train_tfidf, y_train)
```

Step 5: Evaluate the Model
python

```
# Make predictions
y_pred = model.predict(X_test_tfidf)
```

```
# Evaluate performance
print(classification_report(y_test, y_pred))
```

Expected Output

plaintext

	precision	recall	f1-score	support
0	1.00	1.00	1.00	1
1	1.00	1.00	1.00	1
accuracy			1.00	2
macro avg	1.00	1.00	1.00	2
weighted avg	1.00	1.00	1.00	2

In this chapter, we introduced the basics of NLP, its importance in AI, and the steps involved in text preprocessing, including tokenization, stemming, and lemmatization. We explored two popular methods for representing text as numbers: Bag-of-Words and TF-IDF. Finally, we applied these concepts to perform sentiment analysis on customer reviews, demonstrating how to preprocess text, vectorize it, and build a classification model. These foundational skills set the stage for more advanced NLP techniques in upcoming chapters.

CHAPTER 11: RECURRENT NEURAL NETWORKS (RNNS)

Recurrent Neural Networks (RNNs) are designed to process sequential data, such as time-series, text, or audio. Unlike traditional neural networks, RNNs have a memory component that allows them to retain information about previous inputs, making them well-suited for tasks involving context or temporal dependencies. In this chapter, we'll explore the fundamentals of RNNs, discuss key concepts like hidden states and memory cells, and address challenges like the vanishing gradient problem. We'll also demonstrate how to build and train RNNs using TensorFlow and Keras, culminating in a real-world example: **predicting stock prices**.

11.1 Understanding Sequential Data and Why RNNs Are Used

11.1.1 What is Sequential Data?

Sequential data is data where the order of elements matters. Examples include:

- **Time-Series Data**: Stock prices, weather data, sensor readings.
- **Text Data**: Sentences where word order affects meaning.

- **Audio Data**: Speech or music.

11.1.2 Why Use RNNs for Sequential Data?

Traditional neural networks treat each input independently, ignoring temporal dependencies. RNNs address this limitation by:

- Retaining information about previous inputs through hidden states.
- Capturing temporal relationships in sequences.

Example: To predict the next word in a sentence, the network needs to understand the context provided by earlier words.

11.2 Key Concepts of RNNs

11.2.1 Hidden States

- RNNs have a hidden state (hth_tht) that stores information about previous inputs.
- At each time step, the hidden state is updated based on the current input (xtx_txt) and the previous hidden state (ht−1h_{t-1}ht−1).

The update rule:

$$ht=activation(Wxhxt+Whhht−1+bh)h\_t = \text{activation}(W\_{xh} x\_t + W\_{hh} h\_{t-1} + b\_h)ht=activation(Wxhxt+Whhht−1+bh)$$

11.2.2 Memory Cells

Memory cells are mechanisms in RNNs that allow them to "remember" long-term dependencies. They are crucial in advanced RNN architectures like LSTMs (Long Short-Term Memory) and GRUs (Gated Recurrent Units).

11.2.3 Challenges with RNNs

1. **Vanishing Gradient Problem**:
   o Gradients shrink as they are propagated backward through time, causing the model to forget long-term dependencies.
   o Solution: Use LSTMs or GRUs, which mitigate this problem by introducing gating mechanisms.
2. **Exploding Gradient Problem**:
   o Gradients become excessively large, destabilizing the training process.
   o Solution: Gradient clipping.

11.3 Building and Training RNNs with TensorFlow and Keras

Step 1: Import Libraries

python

```python
import numpy as np
import tensorflow as tf
from tensorflow.keras.models import Sequential
from tensorflow.keras.layers import SimpleRNN, Dense
```

Step 2: Prepare Sequential Data

For demonstration, let's generate a sine wave dataset to predict the next value in the sequence.

python

```python
# Generate a sine wave dataset
timesteps = 100
X = np.linspace(0, 100, timesteps)
y = np.sin(X)


# Create input-output pairs
sequence_length = 10
X_data = []
y_data = []


for i in range(len(y) - sequence_length):
    X_data.append(y[i:i+sequence_length])
    y_data.append(y[i+sequence_length])
```

```
X_data = np.array(X_data)
y_data = np.array(y_data)
```

```
# Reshape data for RNN
X_data = X_data.reshape((X_data.shape[0], X_data.shape[1], 1))
```

Step 3: Build the RNN Model
python

```
# Define the RNN model
model = Sequential([
    SimpleRNN(50,                                activation='relu',
input_shape=(sequence_length, 1)),
    Dense(1)  # Output layer
])
```

Step 4: Compile the Model
python

```
# Compile the model
model.compile(optimizer='adam', loss='mse', metrics=['mae'])
```

Step 5: Train the Model
python

```
# Train the model
history = model.fit(X_data, y_data, epochs=50, batch_size=16,
validation_split=0.2)
```

Step 6: Evaluate the Model
python

```
# Evaluate performance
loss, mae = model.evaluate(X_data, y_data)
print(f"Loss: {loss}, Mean Absolute Error: {mae}")
```

11.4 Real-World Example: Predicting Stock Prices Using RNNs

Problem Statement
Predict future stock prices based on historical data using an RNN.

Step 1: Load and Preprocess Data
python

```
import pandas as pd
from sklearn.preprocessing import MinMaxScaler
```

```python
# Load stock price data
df = pd.read_csv('stock_prices.csv')

# Use the "Close" column as the target
prices = df['Close'].values

# Normalize data
scaler = MinMaxScaler()
prices = scaler.fit_transform(prices.reshape(-1, 1))

# Prepare sequential data
sequence_length = 50
X_data = []
y_data = []

for i in range(len(prices) - sequence_length):
    X_data.append(prices[i:i+sequence_length])
    y_data.append(prices[i+sequence_length])

X_data = np.array(X_data)
y_data = np.array(y_data)

# Reshape for RNN input
X_data = X_data.reshape((X_data.shape[0], X_data.shape[1], 1))
```

Step 2: Build the RNN Model
python

```
from tensorflow.keras.layers import LSTM

# Define the RNN model
model = Sequential([
    LSTM(100,        activation='relu',        return_sequences=False,
input_shape=(sequence_length, 1)),
    Dense(1)  # Output layer
])
```

Step 3: Compile and Train the Model
python

```
# Compile the model
model.compile(optimizer='adam', loss='mse')

# Train the model
history = model.fit(X_data, y_data, epochs=20, batch_size=32,
validation_split=0.2)
```

Step 4: Make Predictions
python

```python
# Predict the next value
test_sequence = X_data[-1].reshape(1, sequence_length, 1)
predicted_price = model.predict(test_sequence)

# Reverse scaling
predicted_price = scaler.inverse_transform(predicted_price)
print(f"Predicted Price: {predicted_price[0][0]}")
```

Step 5: Visualize Predictions
python

```python
import matplotlib.pyplot as plt

# Predict the entire sequence
y_pred = model.predict(X_data)

# Reverse scaling
y_pred = scaler.inverse_transform(y_pred)
y_actual = scaler.inverse_transform(y_data.reshape(-1, 1))

# Plot results
plt.plot(y_actual, label="Actual Prices")
plt.plot(y_pred, label="Predicted Prices")
plt.legend()
```

plt.show()

Analysis of Results

- **Expected Outcome**: The RNN should capture short-term trends in the stock prices.
- **Challenges**: Stock prices are influenced by numerous factors; combining RNNs with external features (e.g., news sentiment) can improve predictions.

Recurrent Neural Networks are powerful tools for modeling sequential data, enabling tasks like time-series prediction, text analysis, and speech recognition. This chapter explained the fundamental concepts of RNNs, including hidden states, memory cells, and their challenges, like the vanishing gradient problem. Using TensorFlow and Keras, we built RNN models to predict sequential data and applied these skills to a real-world example of stock price prediction. In the following chapters, you'll explore advanced RNN variants like LSTMs and GRUs, further enhancing your ability to tackle complex sequential data tasks.

CHAPTER 12: LONG SHORT-TERM MEMORY (LSTM) AND GRU

Recurrent Neural Networks (RNNs) are powerful for sequential data, but they struggle with long-term dependencies due to issues like vanishing gradients. Long Short-Term Memory (LSTM) and Gated Recurrent Unit (GRU) networks address these limitations, enabling better handling of longer sequences. In this chapter, we'll discuss the shortcomings of RNNs, explore the mechanisms of LSTMs and GRUs, and guide you in choosing the right architecture for your problem. Finally, we'll implement a real-world example: **generating text using LSTMs**.

12.1 Limitations of RNNs and How LSTMs and GRUs Solve Them

12.1.1 Limitations of RNNs

1. **Vanishing Gradients**:
   - As gradients backpropagate through many time steps, they diminish exponentially, making it hard for the network to learn long-term dependencies.
2. **Short-Term Memory**:

o RNNs prioritize recent inputs and struggle to remember earlier ones in long sequences.

3. **Training Challenges**:

   o RNNs are slower to train due to sequential processing of data.

12.1.2 How LSTMs and GRUs Solve These Issues

LSTMs and GRUs introduce gating mechanisms that regulate the flow of information, allowing networks to selectively retain or discard information over long sequences.

Key Features:

- **Memory Cells**: Store information over long durations.
- **Gates**: Control the flow of information, deciding what to keep or forget.

12.2 Components of LSTMs

LSTMs use three main gates to manage memory and retain important features over time:

1. **Forget Gate**:

- o Decides what information to discard from the memory cell.
- o Formula: $f_t = \sigma(W_f \cdot [h_{t-1}, x_t] + b_f)$
- o f_t: Forget gate activation.

2. **Input Gate**:
   - o Decides what new information to add to the memory cell.
   - o Formula: $i_t = \sigma(W_i \cdot [h_{t-1}, x_t] + b_i)$
     $\tilde{C}_t = \tanh(W_C \cdot [h_{t-1}, x_t] + b_C)$
     $C_t = f_t \cdot C_{t-1} + i_t \cdot \tilde{C}_t$
   - o i_t: Input gate activation, $\tilde{C}_t$: Candidate memory.

3. **Output Gate**:
   - o Determines the output based on the memory cell.
   - o Formula: $o_t = \sigma(W_o \cdot [h_{t-1}, x_t] + b_o)$
     $h_t = o_t \cdot \tanh(C_t)$
   - o o_t: Output gate activation.

12.3 GRUs: A Simpler Alternative

Gated Recurrent Units (GRUs) simplify LSTMs by combining the forget and input gates into a single update gate. They have fewer parameters, making them faster to train while maintaining similar performance for many tasks.

Key Equations:

1. **Update Gate**: zt=σ(Wz·[ht−1,xt]+bz)z_t = \sigma(W_z \cdot [h_{t-1}, x_t] + b_z)zt=σ(Wz·[ht−1,xt]+bz)

2. **Reset Gate**: rt=σ(Wr·[ht−1,xt]+br)r_t = \sigma(W_r \cdot [h_{t-1}, x_t] + b_r)rt=σ(Wr·[ht−1,xt]+br)

3. **Current Memory**: h~t=tanh⁡(W·[rt·ht−1,xt]+b)\tilde{h}_t = \tanh(W \cdot [r_t \cdot h_{t-1}, x_t] + b)h~t=tanh(W·[rt·ht−1,xt]+b)

4. **Final Output**: ht=zt·ht−1+(1−zt)·h~th_t = z_t \cdot h_{t-1} + (1 - z_t) \cdot \tilde{h}_tht=zt·ht−1+(1−zt)·h~t

12.4 Choosing Between LSTMs and GRUs

Aspect	LSTM	GRU

Aspect	LSTM	GRU
Complexity	More complex with three gates.	Simpler with two gates.
Performance	Better for very long sequences.	Similar performance for many tasks.
Training Speed	Slower due to more parameters.	Faster with fewer parameters.
Memory Usage	Higher memory requirements.	Lower memory requirements.

Recommendation:

- Use **LSTMs** for tasks requiring precise long-term memory (e.g., language modeling).
- Use **GRUs** for faster training and tasks with less complex dependencies.

12.5 Real-World Example: Generating Text Using LSTMs

Problem Statement

Build a model that generates text based on a given input sequence. For this example, we'll use a dataset of famous quotes.

Step 1: Import Libraries

python

```
import numpy as np
from tensorflow.keras.models import Sequential
from tensorflow.keras.layers import LSTM, Dense
from tensorflow.keras.preprocessing.text import Tokenizer
from tensorflow.keras.utils import to_categorical
```

Step 2: Prepare the Data

python

```
# Sample dataset
data = """The journey of a thousand miles begins with one step.
    Life is what happens when you're busy making other plans.
    To be yourself in a world that is constantly trying to make
you something else is the greatest accomplishment."""

# Tokenize text
tokenizer = Tokenizer()
tokenizer.fit_on_texts([data])
total_words = len(tokenizer.word_index) + 1
```

```
# Convert text to sequences
input_sequences = []
for line in data.split("\n"):
    tokens = tokenizer.texts_to_sequences([line.strip()])[0]
    for i in range(1, len(tokens)):
        input_sequences.append(tokens[:i+1])


# Pad sequences
max_sequence_len = max([len(seq) for seq in input_sequences])
input_sequences = np.array([np.pad(seq, (0, max_sequence_len - len(seq))) for seq in input_sequences])


# Split into predictors and labels
X, y = input_sequences[:, :-1], input_sequences[:, -1]
y = to_categorical(y, num_classes=total_words)
```

Step 3: Build the LSTM Model
python

```
model = Sequential([
    LSTM(150, input_shape=(X.shape[1], X.shape[2]), return_sequences=True),
    LSTM(150),
    Dense(total_words, activation='softmax')
])
```

```python
model.compile(optimizer='adam', loss='categorical_crossentropy', metrics=['accuracy'])
```

Step 4: Train the Model
python

```python
model.fit(X, y, epochs=50, verbose=1)
```

Step 5: Generate Text
python

```python
def generate_text(seed_text, next_words, max_sequence_len):
    for _ in range(next_words):
        token_list = tokenizer.texts_to_sequences([seed_text])[0]
        token_list = np.pad(token_list, (0, max_sequence_len - len(token_list)))
        predicted = np.argmax(model.predict(token_list.reshape(1, max_sequence_len, 1)))
        for word, index in tokenizer.word_index.items():
            if index == predicted:
                seed_text += " " + word
                break
    return seed_text
```

```
seed_text = "Life is"
print(generate_text(seed_text, 5, max_sequence_len))
```

Expected Output

plaintext

Life is what happens when you're busy

Analysis of Results

- The model generates coherent text based on the input sequence.
- Increasing training data or using pre-trained embeddings (e.g., GloVe) can further improve quality.

This chapter introduced LSTMs and GRUs as solutions to the limitations of traditional RNNs. We examined the gating mechanisms that enable these architectures to retain long-term dependencies and discussed how to choose between them. Through a real-world example of text generation, we demonstrated how to preprocess text, build an LSTM-based model, and generate meaningful sequences. These techniques are foundational for advanced NLP tasks like machine translation, chatbots, and summarization.

CHAPTER 13: ATTENTION MECHANISMS AND TRANSFORMERS

Deep learning has been revolutionized by attention mechanisms and transformers, particularly in the field of natural language processing (NLP). Attention mechanisms allow models to focus on the most relevant parts of the input, while transformers have replaced traditional recurrent architectures for their efficiency and scalability. In this chapter, we'll discuss attention, explore transformer architectures, introduce BERT and GPT, and implement a real-world example of **text summarization using transformers**.

13.1 Understanding Attention in Deep Learning

13.1.1 What is Attention?

Attention is a mechanism that enables models to selectively focus on different parts of the input sequence while making predictions. It allows the model to weigh the importance of each input token dynamically.

Example:

- In machine translation, attention helps the model align input words (e.g., "je t'aime") with their corresponding output words (e.g., "I love you").

13.1.2 How Attention Works

1. **Query, Key, and Value**:
   - Each input token is projected into three vectors:
     - **Query** (QQQ): What the model is searching for.
     - **Key** (KKK): Features associated with each token.
     - **Value** (VVV): Information to retrieve.

2. **Attention Score**:
   - Compute the similarity between the query and all keys:

     Attention Score=softmax(Q·KTdk)\text{Attention Score} = \text{softmax} \left(\frac{Q \cdot K^T}{\sqrt{d_k}} \right)Attention Score=softmax(dkQ·KT)

3. **Weighted Summation**:
   - Use the attention scores to weight the values:

     Attention Output=Scores·V\text{Attention Output} = \text{Scores} \cdot VAttention Output=Scores·V

Key Properties:

- Attention is **differentiable**, making it trainable with backpropagation.
- It handles long-range dependencies more effectively than recurrent models.

13.2 The Role of Transformers in NLP and Beyond

13.2.1 What are Transformers?

Transformers are deep learning architectures built entirely on attention mechanisms, replacing recurrence and convolution. They were introduced in the seminal paper *Attention Is All You Need* by Vaswani et al.

13.2.2 Components of a Transformer

1. **Encoder-Decoder Structure**:
    - o **Encoder**: Encodes the input sequence into context-aware embeddings.
    - o **Decoder**: Generates the output sequence, using encoder outputs and attention.
2. **Multi-Head Self-Attention**:
    - o Allows the model to focus on different parts of the input simultaneously.
3. **Positional Encoding**:

o Adds positional information to input embeddings, enabling the model to consider word order.

4. **Feedforward Layers**:

   o Fully connected layers applied after attention to process embeddings further.

13.2.3 Advantages of Transformers

- **Parallelization**: Process entire sequences simultaneously.
- **Scalability**: Handle large datasets efficiently.
- **Versatility**: Used in NLP, vision (e.g., Vision Transformers), and beyond.

13.3 Introduction to BERT and GPT Architectures

13.3.1 BERT (Bidirectional Encoder Representations from Transformers)

- **Key Features**:

  o **Bidirectional Attention**: Considers context from both left and right of each token.

  o **Masked Language Modeling**: Predicts missing words in a sentence.

- o **Next Sentence Prediction**: Determines whether two sentences are consecutive.
- **Applications**:
  - o Text classification, question answering, and sentiment analysis.

13.3.2 GPT (Generative Pre-trained Transformer)

- **Key Features**:
  - o **Autoregressive Model**: Generates text token by token using left-to-right context.
  - o Optimized for language generation tasks.
- **Applications**:
  - o Text generation, summarization, and conversational AI.

13.4 Real-World Example: Text Summarization Using Transformers

Problem Statement

Generate concise summaries for long articles using a pre-trained transformer model.

Step 1: Install Hugging Face Transformers Library

bash

```
pip install transformers
```

Step 2: Import Libraries
python

```
from transformers import pipeline
```

Step 3: Load a Pre-Trained Model for Summarization
python

```
# Load a summarization pipeline
summarizer = pipeline("summarization", model="facebook/bart-large-cnn")
```

Step 4: Define the Input Text
python

```
# Long article text
text = """
Artificial intelligence (AI) is a branch of computer science that aims to create machines
```

DEEP LEARNING FOR BEGINNERS

capable of intelligent behavior. It has applications in various industries, including healthcare,

finance, and transportation. Machine learning, a subset of AI, allows computers to learn from data

without explicit programming. Recent advancements in AI, such as natural language processing and

computer vision, are transforming how humans interact with technology. However, ethical concerns

regarding AI's impact on jobs and privacy continue to be debated globally.
"""

Step 5: Generate the Summary
python

```
# Generate summary
summary = summarizer(text, max_length=50, min_length=25, do_sample=False)
print("Summary:", summary[0]['summary_text'])
```

Expected Output
plaintext

Summary: Artificial intelligence (AI) is a branch of computer science

that aims to create machines capable of intelligent behavior. Recent

advancements in AI are transforming how humans interact with technology.

Step 6: Analyze and Evaluate

1. **Length Control**:
   - Adjust max_length and min_length to modify summary size.
2. **Relevance**:
   - Evaluate the quality of generated summaries for consistency and focus.

13.5 Applications of Transformers Beyond NLP

1. **Vision Transformers (ViT)**:
   - Apply transformer architectures to image recognition tasks.
2. **Speech Processing**:
   - Used for speech-to-text and text-to-speech systems.
3. **Reinforcement Learning**:

    o   Combine transformers with RL for advanced AI agents (e.g., AlphaStar).

Attention mechanisms and transformers have transformed deep learning, enabling models to handle long-range dependencies with unprecedented efficiency. This chapter covered the fundamentals of attention, explored the architecture of transformers, and introduced key models like BERT and GPT. Through a real-world example of text summarization, we demonstrated the practical application of transformers. These tools are foundational for cutting-edge NLP tasks and beyond, offering robust solutions for a wide range of challenges in AI.

CHAPTER 14: WORKING WITH IMAGES IN DEEP LEARNING

Deep learning models have achieved remarkable success in image processing tasks like classification, object detection, and segmentation. This chapter explores techniques for working with image datasets, focusing on data augmentation and preparation. We'll conclude with a real-world example: **building an image classifier for detecting plant diseases.**

14.1 Data Augmentation

14.1.1 What is Data Augmentation?

Data augmentation involves generating variations of images in a dataset to:

- Increase dataset size.
- Improve model generalization.
- Mitigate overfitting.

14.1.2 Techniques for Image Augmentation

1. **Flipping**:
   - Horizontal or vertical flips.
   - Useful when object orientation is not critical.

2. **Rotation**:
   - Rotates images by a certain angle.
   - Helps the model recognize objects from different orientations.

3. **Cropping**:
   - Randomly crops parts of the image.
   - Ensures the model learns from partial information.

4. **Scaling**:
   - Resizes images while maintaining aspect ratio.
   - Useful for multi-scale detection.

5. **Color Jittering**:
   - Randomly adjusts brightness, contrast, and saturation.
   - Simulates lighting variations.

6. **Noise Injection**:
   - Adds random noise to images.
   - Improves robustness to noisy environments.

Code Example:

python

```python
from tensorflow.keras.preprocessing.image import ImageDataGenerator

# Define data augmentation
datagen = ImageDataGenerator(
    rotation_range=20,
    width_shift_range=0.2,
    height_shift_range=0.2,
    shear_range=0.2,
    zoom_range=0.2,
    horizontal_flip=True,
    fill_mode='nearest'
)

# Apply augmentation to a sample image
from tensorflow.keras.utils import img_to_array, load_img
import matplotlib.pyplot as plt

img = load_img('sample_image.jpg')  # Load image
x = img_to_array(img)  # Convert to array
x = x.reshape((1,) + x.shape)  # Reshape for generator

# Generate augmented images
```

```
for    i,    augmented_img    in    enumerate(datagen.flow(x,
batch_size=1)):
    plt.figure(i)
    plt.imshow(augmented_img[0] / 255.0)  # Normalize for display
    if i == 3:  # Display 4 samples
        break
plt.show()
```

14.2 Preparing Image Datasets for Deep Learning

14.2.1 Organizing Datasets

Organize images into directories for training, validation, and testing. A typical structure:

bash

```
dataset/
    train/
        class_1/
        class_2/
    validation/
        class_1/
        class_2/
    test/
        class_1/
```

class_2/

14.2.2 Loading and Preprocessing Images

1. **Loading Images**: Use tools like ImageDataGenerator or tf.data.Dataset for efficient image loading.
2. **Rescaling Pixel Values**: Normalize pixel values to a range of [0, 1] for better model convergence.

python

```
datagen = ImageDataGenerator(rescale=1.0/255.0)
```

3. **Splitting Data**: Ensure a clear separation between training, validation, and test sets.
4. **Batching**: Process images in batches to optimize memory usage.

14.2.3 Tools for Image Data

- **TensorFlow's ImageDataGenerator**: Built-in support for loading, augmenting, and preprocessing images.
- **tf.data.Dataset**: Provides more customization and efficiency for large datasets.

14.3 Real-World Example: Building an Image Classifier for Detecting Plant Diseases

Problem Statement

Build a model to classify images of plant leaves into categories such as healthy or diseased.

Step 1: Import Libraries

python

```python
import tensorflow as tf
from tensorflow.keras.models import Sequential
from tensorflow.keras.layers import Conv2D, MaxPooling2D, Flatten, Dense, Dropout
from tensorflow.keras.preprocessing.image import ImageDataGenerator
```

Step 2: Organize and Augment Data

python

```python
# Define data generators
train_datagen = ImageDataGenerator(
    rescale=1.0/255.0,
    rotation_range=20,
    width_shift_range=0.2,
    height_shift_range=0.2,
    shear_range=0.2,
    zoom_range=0.2,
```

```python
    horizontal_flip=True,
    validation_split=0.2  # Split for validation
)


train_generator = train_datagen.flow_from_directory(
    'dataset/train/',
    target_size=(150, 150),
    batch_size=32,
    class_mode='binary',
    subset='training'  # Use the training subset
)


validation_generator = train_datagen.flow_from_directory(
    'dataset/train/',
    target_size=(150, 150),
    batch_size=32,
    class_mode='binary',
    subset='validation'  # Use the validation subset
)
```

Step 3: Define the CNN Model
python

```python
model = Sequential([
    Conv2D(32, (3, 3), activation='relu', input_shape=(150, 150, 3)),
```

```
    MaxPooling2D((2, 2)),
    Conv2D(64, (3, 3), activation='relu'),
    MaxPooling2D((2, 2)),
    Conv2D(128, (3, 3), activation='relu'),
    MaxPooling2D((2, 2)),
    Flatten(),
    Dense(128, activation='relu'),
    Dropout(0.5),  # Regularization
    Dense(1, activation='sigmoid')  # Binary classification
])
```

Step 4: Compile the Model

python

```
model.compile(optimizer='adam',          loss='binary_crossentropy',
metrics=['accuracy'])
```

Step 5: Train the Model

python

```
history = model.fit(
    train_generator,
    epochs=20,
    validation_data=validation_generator
```

)

Step 6: Evaluate the Model

python

```python
# Evaluate on test data
test_datagen = ImageDataGenerator(rescale=1.0/255.0)
test_generator = test_datagen.flow_from_directory(
    'dataset/test/',
    target_size=(150, 150),
    batch_size=32,
    class_mode='binary'
)

loss, accuracy = model.evaluate(test_generator)
print(f"Test Loss: {loss}, Test Accuracy: {accuracy}")
```

Step 7: Make Predictions

python

```python
# Predict on a new image
import numpy as np
from tensorflow.keras.preprocessing.image import load_img, img_to_array
```

```
img = load_img('dataset/sample_leaf.jpg', target_size=(150, 150))
img_array = img_to_array(img) / 255.0  # Normalize
img_array = np.expand_dims(img_array, axis=0)   # Add batch dimension

prediction = model.predict(img_array)
print("Predicted Class:", "Healthy" if prediction[0][0] < 0.5 else "Diseased")
```

Analysis of Results

1. **Expected Accuracy**:
   o With sufficient data, the model should achieve >90% accuracy for binary classification tasks.
2. **Challenges**:
   o Imbalanced datasets may lead to biased predictions; address this with data augmentation or class weights.

This chapter introduced essential techniques for working with images in deep learning, including data augmentation and preprocessing. We applied these concepts in a real-world task: building a CNN to classify plant diseases. The combination of data augmentation, proper dataset organization, and a well-designed

CNN allows the model to generalize effectively. These skills are foundational for tackling a wide range of computer vision challenges.

CHAPTER 15: OBJECT DETECTION WITH DEEP LEARNING

Object detection combines classification and localization to identify objects in an image and draw bounding boxes around them. This chapter explores the fundamentals of object detection, introduces popular models like YOLO and Faster R-CNN, and walks you through building an object detection pipeline. We'll conclude with a real-world example: **detecting traffic signs in real-time.**

15.1 Understanding Object Detection

15.1.1 What is Object Detection?

Object detection identifies objects in an image and provides:

- **Class Labels**: The category of each detected object.
- **Bounding Boxes**: Coordinates defining the region of the image containing the object.

15.1.2 Applications of Object Detection

- **Autonomous Vehicles**: Detecting pedestrians, traffic signs, and other vehicles.
- **Security Systems**: Identifying intruders or suspicious activities.
- **Retail Analytics**: Tracking customer behavior and inventory.

15.1.3 Key Components of Object Detection

1. **Feature Extraction**:
   o Extract meaningful patterns from the input image using convolutional layers.
2. **Region Proposal**:
   o Identify regions likely to contain objects.
3. **Classification and Localization**:
   o Predict the object class and refine bounding box coordinates.

15.2 Popular Object Detection Models

15.2.1 YOLO (You Only Look Once)

- **Key Features**:
  - o Divides the image into a grid and predicts bounding boxes and class probabilities directly.
  - o Real-time performance with high speed.
- **Advantages**:
  - o Fast and efficient for real-time applications.
  - o Single forward pass for detection.
- **Use Case**: Traffic monitoring, real-time video processing.

15.2.2 Faster R-CNN (Region-Based Convolutional Neural Network)

- **Key Features**:
  - o Combines region proposal and object classification into a single network.
  - o Generates region proposals using a Region Proposal Network (RPN).
- **Advantages**:

- o High accuracy for complex images with multiple objects.
- o Suitable for applications requiring precision.
- **Use Case**: Medical imaging, security systems.

15.3 Building an Object Detection Pipeline

An object detection pipeline includes the following steps:

15.3.1 Data Preparation

1. **Annotating Images**:
   - o Label images with bounding boxes and class labels using tools like LabelImg.
   - o Save annotations in formats like Pascal VOC or COCO JSON.
2. **Dataset Splitting**:
   - o Divide the dataset into training, validation, and test sets.

15.3.2 Model Selection

Choose a model based on your requirements:

- **YOLO**: For speed and real-time applications.
- **Faster R-CNN**: For high accuracy.

15.3.3 Training the Model

1. **Pretrained Weights**:
   - Start with pretrained weights (e.g., COCO dataset) for transfer learning.
2. **Fine-Tuning**:
   - Fine-tune the model on your dataset by adjusting parameters like learning rate and batch size.

15.3.4 Evaluation

Evaluate the model using metrics like:

- **Mean Average Precision (mAP)**: Measures precision across multiple classes and IoU thresholds.
- **IoU (Intersection over Union)**: Evaluates overlap between predicted and ground-truth bounding boxes.

15.4 Real-World Example: Detecting Traffic Signs in Real-Time

Problem Statement

Develop a model to detect and classify traffic signs in real-time using a webcam or video stream.

Step 1: Install Required Libraries

bash

```
pip install tensorflow opencv-python
```

Step 2: Load a Pre-Trained YOLO Model

Use a pre-trained YOLO model (e.g., YOLOv3) for simplicity.

python

```
import cv2
import numpy as np

# Load YOLO model
net = cv2.dnn.readNet("yolov3.weights", "yolov3.cfg")

# Load class labels
with open("coco.names", "r") as f:
    classes = [line.strip() for line in f.readlines()]
```

```python
# Set up output layers
layer_names = net.getLayerNames()
output_layers = [layer_names[i[0] - 1] for i in net.getUnconnectedOutLayers()]
```

Step 3: Define the Detection Function
python

```python
def detect_objects(image):
    height, width, _ = image.shape

    # Create blob from image
    blob = cv2.dnn.blobFromImage(image, 0.00392, (416, 416), (0, 0, 0), True, crop=False)
    net.setInput(blob)

    # Run forward pass
    outs = net.forward(output_layers)

    # Process detections
    boxes, confidences, class_ids = [], [], []
    for out in outs:
        for detection in out:
            scores = detection[5:]
            class_id = np.argmax(scores)
```

```
            confidence = scores[class_id]

        # Filter by confidence
        if confidence > 0.5:
            center_x, center_y, w, h = (detection[0:4] * [width,
height, width, height]).astype("int")
            x, y = int(center_x - w / 2), int(center_y - h / 2)
            boxes.append([x, y, int(w), int(h)])
            confidences.append(float(confidence))
            class_ids.append(class_id)

    # Non-Maximum Suppression
    indices = cv2.dnn.NMSBoxes(boxes, confidences, 0.5, 0.4)
    for i in indices:
        i = i[0]
        x, y, w, h = boxes[i]
        label = f"{classes[class_ids[i]]}: {int(confidences[i] *
100)}%"
        color = (0, 255, 0)
        cv2.rectangle(image, (x, y), (x + w, y + h), color, 2)
        cv2.putText(image, label, (x, y - 10),
cv2.FONT_HERSHEY_SIMPLEX, 0.5, color, 2)

    return image
```

Step 4: Run Real-Time Detection

python

```python
# Open video stream
cap = cv2.VideoCapture(0)

while True:
    ret, frame = cap.read()
    if not ret:
        break

    # Detect objects
    detected_frame = detect_objects(frame)

    # Display results
    cv2.imshow("Traffic Sign Detection", detected_frame)

    if cv2.waitKey(1) & 0xFF == ord("q"):
        break

cap.release()
cv2.destroyAllWindows()
```

15.5 Analysis and Insights

Expected Outcomes

- The model should detect and classify traffic signs (e.g., stop signs, speed limits) with bounding boxes and confidence scores in real-time.

Challenges and Improvements

1. **Low Accuracy**:
   o Fine-tune the model on a traffic sign-specific dataset (e.g., GTSRB).
2. **Performance Bottlenecks**:
   o Use a GPU for faster inference.
3. **Edge Cases**:
   o Handle occluded or partially visible signs with better training data.

This chapter introduced object detection, explained its key components, and covered popular models like YOLO and Faster R-CNN. Through a real-world example of detecting traffic signs in real-time, we demonstrated how to build and deploy an object detection pipeline. Object detection has wide-ranging applications across industries, and mastering these techniques equips you to tackle complex challenges in computer vision.

CHAPTER 16: GENERATIVE ADVERSARIAL NETWORKS (GANS)

Generative Adversarial Networks (GANs) are an exciting development in deep learning, enabling the generation of realistic synthetic data. GANs consist of two neural networks—the generator and the discriminator—that compete against each other to improve their performance. In this chapter, we'll explore the fundamentals of GANs, their applications, and the process of building a simple GAN using TensorFlow. Finally, we'll implement a real-world example of **generating synthetic images for data augmentation**.

16.1 Introduction to GANs: Generators and Discriminators

16.1.1 What are GANs?

A GAN is a framework comprising two neural networks:

1. **Generator**:
   - Generates synthetic data from random noise.
   - Learns to mimic the real data distribution.
2. **Discriminator**:
   - Evaluates whether the input data is real or synthetic.
   - Guides the generator to produce more realistic outputs.

Adversarial Training:

- The generator tries to fool the discriminator by producing realistic data.
- The discriminator tries to correctly distinguish between real and synthetic data.
- This adversarial process improves both networks over time.

16.1.2 How GANs Work

1. **Input Noise**:

   o The generator takes random noise (e.g., Gaussian distribution) as input.

2. **Generated Output**:

   o The generator creates synthetic data (e.g., an image).

3. **Discriminator Evaluation**:

   o The discriminator evaluates whether the data is real or generated.

4. **Feedback**:

   o The discriminator provides feedback to the generator to improve the quality of the synthetic data.

16.2 Applications of GANs

GANs have diverse applications, including:

1. **Image Generation**:

   o Generate realistic images (e.g., faces, landscapes).

   o Example: DeepFake technology.

2. **Style Transfer**:

   o Convert images to specific artistic styles (e.g., Van Gogh-style paintings).

3. **Data Augmentation**:

   o Create synthetic data to supplement limited datasets.

4. **Super-Resolution**:

o   Enhance image resolution.

5. **Drug Discovery**:

o   Generate molecular structures for potential drugs.

16.3 Building a Simple GAN with TensorFlow

16.3.1 Import Libraries
python

```
import tensorflow as tf
from tensorflow.keras import Sequential
from tensorflow.keras.layers import Dense, LeakyReLU, Reshape,
Flatten
import numpy as np
import matplotlib.pyplot as plt
```

16.3.2 Define the Generator
The generator takes random noise as input and produces synthetic data.

python

```
def build_generator(latent_dim):
    model = Sequential([
        Dense(128, input_dim=latent_dim),
        LeakyReLU(alpha=0.2),
```

```
    Dense(256),

    LeakyReLU(alpha=0.2),

    Dense(512),

    LeakyReLU(alpha=0.2),

    Dense(28 * 28, activation='tanh'),   # Output shape matches
the image size

    Reshape((28, 28))

  ])

  return model
```

16.3.3 Define the Discriminator

The discriminator evaluates whether an input image is real or generated.

python

```
def build_discriminator():
    model = Sequential([
      Flatten(input_shape=(28, 28)),
      Dense(512),
      LeakyReLU(alpha=0.2),
      Dense(256),
      LeakyReLU(alpha=0.2),
      Dense(1, activation='sigmoid')  # Outputs probability
    ])
```

```
    return model
```

16.3.4 Compile the Models

python

```
latent_dim = 100  # Dimension of the random noise vector

# Build and compile the discriminator
discriminator = build_discriminator()
discriminator.compile(optimizer='adam',
loss='binary_crossentropy', metrics=['accuracy'])

# Build the generator
generator = build_generator(latent_dim)

# Combine generator and discriminator
discriminator.trainable = False    # Freeze discriminator during
generator training
gan = Sequential([generator, discriminator])
gan.compile(optimizer='adam', loss='binary_crossentropy')
```

16.3.5 Training the GAN

1. Generate random noise.
2. Create synthetic images using the generator.

3. Train the discriminator on real and synthetic images.

4. Train the generator using the combined GAN model.

python

```python
# Load and preprocess the dataset
(X_train, _), (_, _) = tf.keras.datasets.mnist.load_data()
X_train = (X_train - 127.5) / 127.5  # Normalize to [-1, 1]
X_train = np.expand_dims(X_train, axis=-1)   # Add channel dimension

batch_size = 128
epochs = 10000

# Training loop
for epoch in range(epochs):
    # Train discriminator
    idx = np.random.randint(0, X_train.shape[0], batch_size)
    real_images = X_train[idx]
    noise = np.random.normal(0, 1, (batch_size, latent_dim))
    fake_images = generator.predict(noise)

    real_labels = np.ones((batch_size, 1))
    fake_labels = np.zeros((batch_size, 1))
```

DEEP LEARNING FOR BEGINNERS

```python
    d_loss_real     =     discriminator.train_on_batch(real_images,
real_labels)
    d_loss_fake     =     discriminator.train_on_batch(fake_images,
fake_labels)
    d_loss = 0.5 * np.add(d_loss_real, d_loss_fake)

    # Train generator
    noise = np.random.normal(0, 1, (batch_size, latent_dim))
    valid_labels = np.ones((batch_size, 1))  # The generator wants
its outputs to be classified as real
    g_loss = gan.train_on_batch(noise, valid_labels)

    # Print progress
    if epoch % 1000 == 0:
        print(f"Epoch  {epoch}:  D  Loss:  {d_loss[0]},  G  Loss:
{g_loss}")
```

16.3.6 Visualize Generated Images
python

```python
# Generate and plot synthetic images
def        plot_generated_images(generator,        latent_dim,
num_images=10):
    noise = np.random.normal(0, 1, (num_images, latent_dim))
    generated_images = generator.predict(noise)
```

```
generated_images = 0.5 * generated_images + 0.5  # Rescale to
[0, 1]

plt.figure(figsize=(10, 2))
for i in range(num_images):
    plt.subplot(1, num_images, i + 1)
    plt.imshow(generated_images[i], cmap='gray')
    plt.axis('off')
plt.show()

plot_generated_images(generator, latent_dim)
```

16.4 Real-World Example: Generating Synthetic Images for Data Augmentation

Problem Statement

Generate synthetic images of handwritten digits to augment a limited dataset.

Step 1: Generate Synthetic Data

Using the trained generator, create new images to supplement the existing dataset.

python

```
# Generate synthetic images
```

```python
num_images = 1000
noise = np.random.normal(0, 1, (num_images, latent_dim))
synthetic_images = generator.predict(noise)
```

Step 2: Save the Synthetic Data

Save the generated images to disk for later use.

python

```python
import os

output_dir = "synthetic_digits"
os.makedirs(output_dir, exist_ok=True)

for i, img in enumerate(synthetic_images):
    plt.imsave(f"{output_dir}/digit_{i}.png",          img.squeeze(),
cmap='gray')
```

16.5 Analysis and Insights

1. **Realism of Generated Data**:
   o Visual inspection of generated images helps verify quality.
   o Metrics like Fréchet Inception Distance (FID) provide quantitative evaluation.

2. **Applications**:

   ○ Augmented datasets can improve the performance of classifiers trained on small datasets.

3. **Challenges**:

   ○ GAN training is sensitive to hyperparameters and can be unstable.

Generative Adversarial Networks are powerful tools for generating realistic synthetic data, with applications in image generation, style transfer, and data augmentation. This chapter introduced the core concepts of GANs, their applications, and the process of building a simple GAN using TensorFlow. Through a real-world example of generating synthetic handwritten digits, we demonstrated how GANs can augment datasets, providing practical benefits in scenarios with limited data. These techniques open new avenues for creativity and problem-solving in deep learning.

CHAPTER 17: AUTOENCODERS AND DIMENSIONALITY REDUCTION

Autoencoders are a class of neural networks used for unsupervised learning tasks such as dimensionality reduction, feature extraction, and anomaly detection. By encoding data into a compressed representation and then decoding it, autoencoders can learn to capture essential features while discarding noise. This chapter explores the fundamentals of autoencoders, their applications in dimensionality reduction, and demonstrates a real-world example:

using autoencoders for anomaly detection in financial transactions.

17.1 Understanding Autoencoders and Their Use Cases

17.1.1 What are Autoencoders?

Autoencoders are neural networks that learn to map input data to a compressed representation (encoding) and then reconstruct the original data (decoding).

Architecture:

1. **Encoder**:
   o Compresses input data into a lower-dimensional latent space.
   o Captures the most salient features of the data.
2. **Latent Space**:
   o A bottleneck layer that forces the network to learn a compressed representation.
3. **Decoder**:
   o Reconstructs the input data from the latent representation.

Loss Function:

- Measures the difference between the input and reconstructed data (e.g., Mean Squared Error).

17.1.2 Applications of Autoencoders

1. **Dimensionality Reduction**:
   - Reduce high-dimensional data to a lower-dimensional space for visualization or computational efficiency.
2. **Feature Extraction**:
   - Learn compact representations for downstream tasks like classification or clustering.
3. **Anomaly Detection**:
   - Identify deviations from normal data patterns based on reconstruction error.
4. **Denoising**:
   - Remove noise from corrupted data by reconstructing a clean version.
5. **Image Compression**:
   - Compress images into smaller sizes for storage and transmission.

17.2 Reducing Dimensions for Visualization and Feature Extraction

17.2.1 Dimensionality Reduction

Autoencoders can reduce the number of features while retaining critical information, similar to Principal Component Analysis (PCA). However, autoencoders can model non-linear relationships, making them more flexible than PCA.

17.2.2 Feature Extraction

The latent representation learned by the encoder can serve as a compact feature set for tasks like clustering or classification.

Example Workflow:

1. Train an autoencoder on the dataset.
2. Extract the encoder part of the network.
3. Use the encoder to transform input data into features for machine learning models.

17.3 Real-World Example: Using Autoencoders for Anomaly Detection in Financial Transactions

Anomaly detection involves identifying data points that deviate significantly from the norm. Autoencoders are well-suited for this task because they can reconstruct normal data accurately but struggle with anomalous data, resulting in higher reconstruction errors.

Step 1: Import Libraries

python

```
import numpy as np
import pandas as pd
from tensorflow.keras.models import Model, Sequential
from tensorflow.keras.layers import Dense, Input
from sklearn.model_selection import train_test_split
from sklearn.preprocessing import StandardScaler
import matplotlib.pyplot as plt
```

Step 2: Load and Preprocess Data

For this example, assume we have a dataset of financial transactions with features such as amount, time, and type.

python

```
# Load dataset
data = pd.read_csv("financial_transactions.csv")

# Preprocess data
scaler = StandardScaler()
data_scaled = scaler.fit_transform(data)
```

Split into train and test sets

X_train, X_test = train_test_split(data_scaled, test_size=0.2, random_state=42)

Step 3: Build the Autoencoder

The autoencoder will compress the data into a smaller latent space and reconstruct it.

python

```python
# Define autoencoder architecture
input_dim = X_train.shape[1]
encoding_dim = 8  # Latent space dimension

# Encoder
input_layer = Input(shape=(input_dim,))
encoded = Dense(encoding_dim, activation="relu")(input_layer)

# Decoder
decoded = Dense(input_dim, activation="sigmoid")(encoded)

# Autoencoder model
autoencoder = Model(inputs=input_layer, outputs=decoded)
autoencoder.compile(optimizer="adam", loss="mse")
```

Step 4: Train the Autoencoder

Train the autoencoder to reconstruct the input data.

python

```python
# Train autoencoder
history = autoencoder.fit(
    X_train, X_train,
    epochs=50,
    batch_size=32,
    validation_split=0.2
)
```

Step 5: Evaluate Reconstruction Error

Use reconstruction error to distinguish normal transactions from anomalies.

python

```python
# Predict reconstruction
reconstructed_data = autoencoder.predict(X_test)
reconstruction_error = np.mean(np.square(X_test - reconstructed_data), axis=1)

# Plot reconstruction error
plt.hist(reconstruction_error, bins=50, alpha=0.75)
```

```
plt.title("Reconstruction Error")
plt.xlabel("Error")
plt.ylabel("Frequency")
plt.show()
```

Step 6: Detect Anomalies

Set a threshold for reconstruction error to classify anomalies.

python

```
# Define anomaly threshold
threshold = np.percentile(reconstruction_error, 95)  # Top 5% as anomalies

# Identify anomalies
anomalies = reconstruction_error > threshold
print(f"Number of anomalies detected: {np.sum(anomalies)}")
```

Analysis and Insights

1. **Interpretation of Results**:
    - Low reconstruction error indicates normal transactions.
    - High reconstruction error suggests anomalies (e.g., fraudulent transactions).

2. **Fine-Tuning**:

   o Adjust the threshold based on the desired sensitivity and precision.

3. **Advantages**:

   o No need for labeled data; the model learns from the structure of normal transactions.

   o Scalable to high-dimensional datasets.

Autoencoders are powerful tools for dimensionality reduction and feature extraction, offering a flexible alternative to traditional techniques like PCA. By compressing data into a latent representation and reconstructing it, autoencoders can identify anomalies effectively. In this chapter, we demonstrated how to use autoencoders for anomaly detection in financial transactions, a critical task in industries like banking and cybersecurity. These techniques provide a foundation for solving complex, unsupervised learning problems across various domains.

CHAPTER 18: HYPERPARAMETER TUNING

Hyperparameter tuning is a critical step in optimizing deep learning models. While a model's architecture and weights are learned during training, hyperparameters—such as learning rate, batch size, and the number of neurons—are predefined and significantly impact performance. This chapter covers the importance of hyperparameter tuning, popular methods like grid search, random search, and Bayesian optimization, and tools like Keras Tuner. We conclude with a real-world example: **finding the best model for predicting diabetes**.

18.1 Importance of Hyperparameter Tuning in Deep Learning

Hyperparameters control the learning process and model behavior. Improperly chosen values can result in:

- **Underfitting**: Poor performance due to insufficient model capacity or low learning rates.
- **Overfitting**: High training accuracy but poor generalization due to excessive model capacity or inadequate regularization.

18.1.1 Types of Hyperparameters

1. **Model-Specific**:
   o Number of layers, neurons per layer, activation functions.
2. **Optimization-Specific**:
   o Learning rate, batch size, number of epochs.
3. **Regularization-Specific**:
   o Dropout rate, L1/L2 regularization coefficients.

18.1.2 Benefits of Hyperparameter Tuning

- Improves model accuracy and generalization.
- Reduces training time by avoiding poorly configured models.
- Ensures efficient use of computational resources.

18.2 Methods for Hyperparameter Tuning

18.2.1 Grid Search

- Systematically evaluates all possible combinations of hyperparameter values.
- **Advantages**:
    - o Guarantees exploration of all configurations.
- **Disadvantages**:
    - o Computationally expensive, especially for large search spaces.

Code Example:

python

```
from sklearn.model_selection import GridSearchCV
from tensorflow.keras.wrappers.scikit_learn import KerasClassifier

def build_model(optimizer='adam'):
    model = Sequential([
        Dense(64, activation='relu', input_shape=(input_dim,)),
        Dense(32, activation='relu'),
        Dense(1, activation='sigmoid')
    ])
    model.compile(optimizer=optimizer, loss='binary_crossentropy',
metrics=['accuracy'])
```

return model

```
model = KerasClassifier(build_fn=build_model, verbose=0)
param_grid = {'batch_size': [16, 32], 'epochs': [10, 20], 'optimizer': ['adam', 'sgd']}
grid = GridSearchCV(estimator=model, param_grid=param_grid, cv=3)
grid_result = grid.fit(X_train, y_train)
print("Best Params:", grid_result.best_params_)
```

18.2.2 Random Search

- Randomly samples combinations of hyperparameter values.
- **Advantages**:
  - o Efficient for large search spaces.
  - o Often finds good configurations faster than grid search.
- **Disadvantages**:
  - o May miss optimal configurations.

Code Example:

python

```
from sklearn.model_selection import RandomizedSearchCV
```

```python
param_dist = {'batch_size': [16, 32, 64], 'epochs': [10, 20, 30],
'optimizer': ['adam', 'rmsprop', 'sgd']}
random = RandomizedSearchCV(estimator=model,
param_distributions=param_dist, n_iter=10, cv=3,
random_state=42)
random_result = random.fit(X_train, y_train)
print("Best Params:", random_result.best_params_)
```

18.2.3 Bayesian Optimization

- Uses probabilistic models to predict performance and iteratively refine the search.
- **Advantages**:
  - ○ More efficient than grid and random search.
  - ○ Focuses on promising areas of the search space.
- **Disadvantages**:
  - ○ More complex to implement.

Tool: optuna, hyperopt

Code Example with Optuna:

python

import optuna

```
def objective(trial):
    learning_rate = trial.suggest_loguniform('learning_rate', 1e-4,
1e-2)
    batch_size = trial.suggest_int('batch_size', 16, 64)
    optimizer = trial.suggest_categorical('optimizer', ['adam', 'sgd'])

    model = Sequential([
        Dense(64, activation='relu', input_shape=(input_dim,)),
        Dense(1, activation='sigmoid')
    ])
    model.compile(optimizer=optimizer, loss='binary_crossentropy',
metrics=['accuracy'])
    model.fit(X_train, y_train, batch_size=batch_size, epochs=10,
verbose=0)
    loss, accuracy = model.evaluate(X_test, y_test, verbose=0)
    return accuracy

study = optuna.create_study(direction='maximize')
study.optimize(objective, n_trials=10)
print("Best Params:", study.best_params)
```

18.3 Automating Tuning with Keras Tuner

Keras Tuner simplifies hyperparameter tuning for TensorFlow models.

Installation:

bash

pip install keras-tuner

Usage Example:

python

```python
from kerastuner.tuners import RandomSearch

def build_model(hp):
    model = Sequential([
        Dense(hp.Int('units', min_value=32, max_value=128, step=32), activation='relu', input_shape=(input_dim,)),
        Dense(1, activation='sigmoid')
    ])
    model.compile(optimizer=hp.Choice('optimizer', ['adam', 'sgd']), loss='binary_crossentropy', metrics=['accuracy'])
    return model

tuner = RandomSearch(
    build_model,
    objective='val_accuracy',
    max_trials=10,
    executions_per_trial=1,
    directory='my_dir',
```

```
    project_name='diabetes_tuning'
)
```

```
tuner.search(X_train, y_train, validation_split=0.2, epochs=10,
verbose=1)
best_hps = tuner.get_best_hyperparameters(num_trials=1)[0]
print("Best Hyperparameters:", best_hps.values)
```

18.4 Real-World Example: Finding the Best Model for Predicting Diabetes

Step 1: Import Libraries and Data
python

```python
import pandas as pd
from sklearn.model_selection import train_test_split
from sklearn.preprocessing import StandardScaler
from tensorflow.keras.models import Sequential
from tensorflow.keras.layers import Dense

# Load and preprocess dataset
data = pd.read_csv('diabetes.csv')
X = data.drop('Outcome', axis=1)
y = data['Outcome']
```

```python
X_train, X_test, y_train, y_test = train_test_split(X, y,
test_size=0.2, random_state=42)
scaler = StandardScaler()
X_train = scaler.fit_transform(X_train)
X_test = scaler.transform(X_test)
input_dim = X_train.shape[1]
```

Step 2: Define the Tuning Process

Use Keras Tuner to explore different hyperparameters for the diabetes prediction model.

python

```python
from kerastuner.tuners import Hyperband

def build_model(hp):
    model = Sequential([
        Dense(hp.Int('units', min_value=32, max_value=128, step=32), activation='relu', input_shape=(input_dim,)),
        Dense(1, activation='sigmoid')
    ])
    model.compile(
        optimizer=hp.Choice('optimizer', ['adam', 'rmsprop', 'sgd']),
        loss='binary_crossentropy',
        metrics=['accuracy']
```

```
)
    return model

tuner = Hyperband(
    build_model,
    objective='val_accuracy',
    max_epochs=20,
    directory='diabetes_dir',
    project_name='hyperparam_tuning'
)

tuner.search(X_train, y_train, validation_split=0.2, verbose=1)
```

Step 3: Evaluate the Best Model
Retrieve the best hyperparameters and evaluate the tuned model.

python

```
best_hps = tuner.get_best_hyperparameters(num_trials=1)[0]
print("Best Hyperparameters:", best_hps.values)

# Build the best model
best_model = tuner.hypermodel.build(best_hps)
history = best_model.fit(X_train, y_train, validation_split=0.2,
epochs=20, verbose=1)
```

```
# Evaluate on test data
loss, accuracy = best_model.evaluate(X_test, y_test)
print(f"Test Loss: {loss}, Test Accuracy: {accuracy}")
```

18.5 Analysis and Insights

Expected Outcome

- The tuned model achieves higher accuracy and generalization compared to manually selected hyperparameters.

Advantages of Automation

- Saves time by streamlining the tuning process.
- Efficiently explores large hyperparameter spaces.

Challenges

- Computationally expensive for large datasets or deep models.
- Requires careful design of search space and stopping criteria.

Hyperparameter tuning is crucial for optimizing deep learning models, impacting both accuracy and generalization. This chapter introduced common methods like grid search, random search, and Bayesian optimization, and demonstrated the use of Keras Tuner for automating the process. Through the real-world example of diabetes prediction, we highlighted the practical benefits of systematic tuning. These techniques enable you to extract maximum performance from your deep learning models efficiently.

CHAPTER 19: EVALUATING AND DEPLOYING DEEP LEARNING MODELS

Once a deep learning model is trained, the next critical steps are evaluating its performance and deploying it for real-world use. Evaluation ensures that the model performs well across various metrics, while deployment integrates it into a production environment to serve end-users. This chapter covers key evaluation metrics for classification, regression, and ranking tasks, explains how to export and deploy models, and provides a real-world example: **deploying a TensorFlow model as a web API**.

19.1 Metrics for Classification, Regression, and Ranking

19.1.1 Classification Metrics

Evaluation metrics for classification assess how well the model predicts discrete labels.

1. **Accuracy**:
   - Percentage of correctly classified samples.

   Accuracy=Correct PredictionsTotal Predictions\text{Accuracy} = \frac{\text{Correct Predictions}}{\text{Total Predictions}}Accuracy=Total PredictionsCorrect Predictions

2. **Precision and Recall**:
   - **Precision**: Correct positive predictions as a percentage of all positive predictions. Precision=True PositivesTrue Positives+False Positives\text{Precision} = \frac{\text{True Positives}}{\text{True Positives} + \text{False}

Positives}}Precision=True Positives+False Positive sTrue Positives

- o **Recall**: Correct positive predictions as a percentage of actual positives. Recall=True PositivesTrue Positives+False Negativ es\text{Recall} = \frac{\text{True Positives}}{\text{True Positives} + \text{False Negatives}}Recall=True Positives+False Negatives True Positives

3. **F1-Score**:

- o Harmonic mean of precision and recall. F1-Score=2×Precision×RecallPrecision+Recall\text{F1 -Score} = 2 \times \frac{\text{Precision} \times \text{Recall}}{\text{Precision} + \text{Recall}}F1-Score=2×Precision+RecallPrecision×Recall

4. **ROC-AUC**:

- o Measures the trade-off between true positive and false positive rates.

Code Example:

python

```
from sklearn.metrics import classification_report, roc_auc_score

y_pred = model.predict(X_test)
```

```
print(classification_report(y_test, y_pred.round()))
print("ROC-AUC:", roc_auc_score(y_test, y_pred))
```

19.1.2 Regression Metrics

Regression metrics evaluate predictions on continuous data.

1. **Mean Absolute Error (MAE):**
   o Average of absolute differences between predicted and actual values. $\text{MAE} = \frac{\sum |y_i - \hat{y}_i|}{n}$ MAE=n∑|yi−y^i|

2. **Mean Squared Error (MSE):**
   o Average of squared differences between predicted and actual values. $\text{MSE} = \frac{\sum (y_i - \hat{y}_i)^2}{n}$ MSE=n∑(yi−y^i)2

3. **Root Mean Squared Error (RMSE):**
   o Square root of MSE, providing error in the same units as the target variable. $\text{RMSE} = \sqrt{\text{MSE}}$ RMSE=MSE

4. **R-Squared (R²):**
   o Proportion of variance in the target variable explained by the model. $R^2 = 1 - \frac{\sum}{}$

$$(y\_i \quad - \quad \hat{y}\_i)^2\}\{\sum \quad (y\_i \quad - \quad \bar{y})\}^2\}R2 = 1 - \sum(yi - y^-)2\sum(yi - y^i)2$$

Code Example:

python

from sklearn.metrics import mean_absolute_error, mean_squared_error, r2_score

mae = mean_absolute_error(y_test, y_pred)
mse = mean_squared_error(y_test, y_pred)
r2 = r2_score(y_test, y_pred)
print(f"MAE: {mae}, MSE: {mse}, R²: {r2}")

19.1.3 Ranking Metrics

Ranking metrics evaluate models that rank items, such as recommendation systems.

1. **Precision@K**:
   o Fraction of relevant items in the top K recommendations.
2. **Mean Average Precision (MAP)**:
   o Average precision across multiple queries.
3. **Normalized Discounted Cumulative Gain (NDCG)**:

○ Measures ranking quality by penalizing incorrect order of items.

19.2 Exporting and Deploying Models

19.2.1 Exporting Models

Export models in a format compatible with production environments (e.g., TensorFlow SavedModel).

TensorFlow SavedModel:

python

```
# Save the trained model
model.save("my_model")
```

Load the Model:

python

```
from tensorflow.keras.models import load_model

model = load_model("my_model")
```

19.2.2 Deploying Models in Production

1. **Deployment Formats**:

- o Export models as REST APIs or embed them in mobile or web applications.

2. **Serving Platforms**:

   - o **TensorFlow Serving**: For deploying TensorFlow models.
   - o **TorchServe**: For PyTorch models.
   - o **ONNX**: For interoperability between frameworks.

3. **Scalability**:

   - o Use containers (e.g., Docker) and orchestration tools (e.g., Kubernetes) for scaling.

19.3 Real-World Example: Deploying a TensorFlow Model as a Web API

Step 1: Train and Save the Model

Assume we have trained a model to predict diabetes.

python

```
model.save("diabetes_model")
```

Step 2: Install FastAPI for API Deployment

FastAPI is a lightweight framework for building APIs.

bash

pip install fastapi uvicorn tensorflow

Step 3: Create the API Server

Define an API to load the model and serve predictions.

python

```python
from fastapi import FastAPI
from pydantic import BaseModel
from tensorflow.keras.models import load_model
import numpy as np

# Load the model
model = load_model("diabetes_model")

# Define the API app
app = FastAPI()

# Define input schema
class DiabetesInput(BaseModel):
    features: list

@app.post("/predict")
def predict(data: DiabetesInput):
```

```
# Convert input to NumPy array
input_data = np.array(data.features).reshape(1, -1)
# Make prediction
prediction = model.predict(input_data)[0][0]
return {"prediction": prediction}
```

Step 4: Run the API Server

Run the FastAPI server locally.

bash

```
uvicorn main:app --reload
```

Step 5: Test the API

Use tools like Postman or Python requests library to send test requests.

Example Request:

python

```
import requests

url = "http://127.0.0.1:8000/predict"
data = {"features": [6, 148, 72, 35, 0, 33.6, 0.627, 50]}
response = requests.post(url, json=data)
```

```
print(response.json())
```

Step 6: Deploy in Production

1. **Containerize with Docker**:
   o   Create a Dockerfile to package the application.

   dockerfile

   ```
   FROM python:3.8-slim
   COPY . /app
   WORKDIR /app
   RUN pip install -r requirements.txt
   CMD ["uvicorn", "main:app", "--host", "0.0.0.0", "--port", "8000"]
   ```

2. **Deploy with Kubernetes**:
   o   Use Kubernetes to scale and manage the deployment.

19.4 Analysis and Insights

1. **Key Considerations for Deployment**:
   o   Ensure low latency for real-time applications.

DEEP LEARNING FOR BEGINNERS

- o Monitor model performance over time (e.g., concept drift).
- o Use logging and metrics to track API usage and errors.

2. **Scalability**:
   - o Implement load balancing and caching for high-traffic scenarios.

3. **Security**:
   - o Protect APIs with authentication and rate limiting.

This chapter introduced essential evaluation metrics for classification, regression, and ranking tasks, highlighting their importance in measuring model performance. We explored the process of exporting and deploying deep learning models, demonstrating how to deploy a TensorFlow model as a web API using FastAPI. These skills enable you to bridge the gap between training and real-world application, making your models accessible and impactful in production environments.

CHAPTER 20: SCALING DEEP LEARNING WITH CLOUD COMPUTING

Scaling deep learning models for large datasets and complex architectures often requires significant computational resources. Cloud computing platforms like AWS, Google Cloud Platform (GCP), and Microsoft Azure provide scalable infrastructure and tools to meet these demands. This chapter explores how to leverage cloud platforms for training models, distributed training techniques with TensorFlow, and a real-world example: **training a large-scale NLP model in the cloud**.

20.1 Using Cloud Platforms for Training Models

20.1.1 Advantages of Cloud Computing

1. **Scalability**:
   - Easily scale up resources (e.g., GPUs, TPUs) to handle large models and datasets.
2. **Cost Efficiency**:
   - Pay-as-you-go pricing eliminates the need for upfront hardware investments.
3. **Access to Specialized Hardware**:

o Cloud providers offer high-performance GPUs (e.g., NVIDIA A100) and TPUs for deep learning.

4. **Collaboration and Accessibility**:

o Teams can access resources and collaborate remotely.

20.1.2 Key Cloud Platforms

1. **Amazon Web Services (AWS)**:

o **Services**: Amazon SageMaker, EC2 with GPU instances.

o **Special Features**: Automated model deployment with SageMaker.

2. **Google Cloud Platform (GCP)**:

o **Services**: Vertex AI, AI Platform.

o **Special Features**: Access to TPUs and deep integration with TensorFlow.

3. **Microsoft Azure**:

o **Services**: Azure Machine Learning.

o **Special Features**: Support for hybrid cloud setups and integration with enterprise systems.

4. **Other Platforms**:

o **Databricks**: Focused on distributed machine learning with Apache Spark.

o **Kaggle Kernels**: Free, limited resources for quick experiments.

20.1.3 Setting Up Cloud Environments

Example with GCP:

1. **Create a Virtual Machine**:
   - Use the GCP console to create a VM with GPU support.
   - Choose a machine type like n1-standard-4 with a Tesla T4 GPU.

2. **Install Deep Learning Frameworks**:

bash

```
sudo apt update
sudo apt install python3-pip
pip install tensorflow keras
```

3. **Upload Data**:
   - Use Google Cloud Storage (GCS) to upload datasets.

20.2 Distributed Training with TensorFlow

Distributed training enables multiple machines or GPUs to collaborate, reducing training time for large models.

20.2.1 Approaches to Distributed Training

1. **Data Parallelism**:
   o Splits data across multiple devices, with each device processing a subset of the data.
   o Updates are aggregated to synchronize the model.
2. **Model Parallelism**:
   o Splits the model itself across devices, useful for very large models.

20.2.2 TensorFlow's Distributed Strategies

1. **MirroredStrategy**:
   o Synchronizes training across multiple GPUs on a single machine.
2. **MultiWorkerMirroredStrategy**:
   o Synchronizes training across multiple machines.
3. **TPUStrategy**:
   o Optimized for training on TPUs.

Code Example with MirroredStrategy:

python

```
import tensorflow as tf

strategy = tf.distribute.MirroredStrategy()
```

```
with strategy.scope():
    model = tf.keras.Sequential([
        tf.keras.layers.Dense(128,                    activation='relu',
input_shape=(input_dim,)),
        tf.keras.layers.Dense(1, activation='sigmoid')
    ])
    model.compile(optimizer='adam',    loss='binary_crossentropy',
metrics=['accuracy'])

# Train the model
model.fit(X_train, y_train, batch_size=64, epochs=10)
```

20.2.3 Tools for Distributed Training

1. **TensorFlow Distributed Training**:
   o   Native tools for scaling models across devices.
2. **Horovod**:
   o   Framework for distributed deep learning optimized for MPI environments.

20.3 Real-World Example: Training a Large-Scale NLP Model in the Cloud

Problem Statement

Train a BERT-based model for sentiment analysis using distributed GPUs in the cloud.

Step 1: Set Up the Cloud Environment

Platform: Google Cloud Platform (GCP).

1. **Create a Compute Engine VM**:
   o Use a machine type like n1-highmem-8 with 2 NVIDIA Tesla T4 GPUs.
2. **Install Necessary Libraries**:

   bash

   pip install transformers tensorflow

Step 2: Prepare the Data

Download and preprocess a sentiment analysis dataset (e.g., IMDb reviews).

python

from transformers import BertTokenizer
from sklearn.model_selection import train_test_split
import tensorflow as tf

Load dataset

```
(X_data, y_data) = load_imdb_dataset()  # Replace with your data loader
```

```
# Tokenize using BERT tokenizer
tokenizer = BertTokenizer.from_pretrained('bert-base-uncased')
X_data = tokenizer(X_data.tolist(), max_length=128, truncation=True, padding=True, return_tensors="tf")
```

```
# Split data
X_train, X_val, y_train, y_val = train_test_split(X_data, y_data, test_size=0.2, random_state=42)
```

Step 3: Define the Model

Use a pre-trained BERT model with TensorFlow.

python

```
from transformers import TFBertForSequenceClassification

strategy = tf.distribute.MirroredStrategy()  # Use multiple GPUs

with strategy.scope():
    model = TFBertForSequenceClassification.from_pretrained('bert-base-uncased', num_labels=2)
```

```
model.compile(optimizer=tf.keras.optimizers.Adam(learning_rate
=3e-5),
            loss='sparse_categorical_crossentropy',
            metrics=['accuracy'])
```

Step 4: Train the Model
python

```
history = model.fit(
    X_train, y_train,
    validation_data=(X_val, y_val),
    batch_size=64,
    epochs=3
)
```

Step 5: Save and Export the Model
python

```
model.save_pretrained("gs://your-bucket-name/sentiment_model")
```

20.4 Analysis and Insights

1. **Advantages of Distributed Training**:

o Significant reduction in training time for large models.

o Scalability to handle massive datasets and complex architectures.

2. **Challenges**:

o High cloud costs for large-scale training.

o Requires careful synchronization and debugging.

3. **Optimization Tips**:

o Use preemptible VMs to reduce costs.

o Monitor resource utilization to identify bottlenecks.

Cloud computing platforms provide the computational power needed to scale deep learning models efficiently. In this chapter, we explored cloud platforms like AWS, GCP, and Azure, discussed distributed training with TensorFlow, and demonstrated training a large-scale NLP model using BERT in the cloud. These skills empower you to tackle demanding deep learning tasks, ensuring both scalability and efficiency for real-world applications.

CHAPTER 21: ETHICS AND CHALLENGES IN DEEP LEARNING

Deep learning has transformed numerous industries, but its widespread adoption raises critical ethical concerns and challenges. These include model bias, explainability, fairness, and environmental impact. Addressing these issues is essential to ensure responsible AI development and deployment. This chapter explores bias in deep learning models and mitigation strategies, the importance of explainability, and challenges such as energy consumption and dataset limitations. We conclude with a **case study on ensuring fairness in loan approval models.**

21.1 Bias in Deep Learning Models and Ways to Mitigate It

21.1.1 Understanding Bias in Deep Learning

Bias occurs when a model systematically favors certain groups or outcomes due to imbalanced data, flawed assumptions, or societal inequalities. Bias in AI can manifest as:

- **Training Data Bias**:
    - Imbalanced datasets that overrepresent or underrepresent specific groups.
- **Algorithmic Bias**:

- o Models learning patterns that reflect societal stereotypes.
- **Deployment Bias**:
  - o Real-world use of models in contexts different from training.

Examples:

- Gender bias in hiring models.
- Racial bias in facial recognition systems.

21.1.2 Mitigation Strategies

1. **Balanced Datasets**:
   - o Ensure datasets are representative of all demographics.
   - o Use data augmentation to address imbalances.
2. **Bias Testing and Metrics**:
   - o Use fairness metrics like disparate impact ratio and equalized odds.
   - o Regularly evaluate models for biased predictions.
3. **Fairness Constraints**:
   - o Incorporate fairness objectives into the training process.

o   Example: Add penalties for disparities in model predictions across groups.

4. **Adversarial Debiasing**:

   o   Train models to minimize sensitive attribute correlations with predictions.

21.2 Explainability and Interpretability of Deep Learning Models

21.2.1 Importance of Explainability

Deep learning models are often criticized as "black boxes" due to their complexity. Explainability helps:

- **Build Trust**:
  - o   Users are more likely to trust models they understand.
- **Ensure Accountability**:
  - o   Interpretability aids in identifying and correcting errors.
- **Comply with Regulations**:
  - o   Laws like GDPR require explainability in automated decision-making systems.

21.2.2 Methods for Explainability

1. **Feature Importance**:
   - o Identify which input features most influence predictions.
   - o Tools: SHAP (SHapley Additive exPlanations), LIME (Local Interpretable Model-agnostic Explanations).

2. **Visualization**:
   - o Use saliency maps and activation heatmaps for image models.
   - o Example: Highlighting regions of an image that influence a classification.

3. **Simplified Models**:
   - o Use interpretable surrogates (e.g., decision trees) to approximate model behavior.

Code Example:

python

```
import shap

explainer = shap.Explainer(model, X_test)
shap_values = explainer(X_test)
shap.summary_plot(shap_values, X_test)
```

21.3 Challenges in Deep Learning

21.3.1 Energy Consumption

Training deep learning models requires substantial computational power, leading to high energy consumption and carbon emissions.

Mitigation Strategies:

- Optimize model architectures for efficiency (e.g., lightweight models like MobileNet).
- Use energy-efficient hardware (e.g., TPUs).
- Offset emissions with renewable energy credits.

21.3.2 Dataset Limitations

1. **Size**:
   - Many domains lack large labeled datasets.
   - Solution: Use data augmentation, transfer learning, or synthetic data generation.
2. **Quality**:
   - Noisy or biased datasets can lead to unreliable models.
   - Solution: Clean and validate datasets thoroughly.

21.3.3 Fairness and Inclusion

Deep learning models may inadvertently perpetuate or amplify societal inequities.

Solutions:

- Regular audits for fairness.
- Involve diverse stakeholders during model design and evaluation.
- Implement post-deployment monitoring.

21.4 Case Study: Ensuring Fairness in Loan Approval Models

Problem Statement

A bank's loan approval model predicts loan eligibility based on applicant data. However, it disproportionately rejects applications from certain demographics.

Step 1: Analyze Dataset for Bias

Check for imbalances in sensitive attributes (e.g., race, gender, income).

python

```python
import pandas as pd

# Load dataset
data = pd.read_csv("loan_data.csv")

# Check for representation
print(data['gender'].value_counts())
print(data['race'].value_counts())
```

Step 2: Train the Initial Model

Train a basic loan approval model.

python

```python
from sklearn.model_selection import train_test_split
from sklearn.ensemble import RandomForestClassifier
from sklearn.metrics import accuracy_score

# Split data
X = data.drop(['loan_approval', 'gender', 'race'], axis=1)  # Exclude sensitive attributes
y = data['loan_approval']
X_train, X_test, y_train, y_test = train_test_split(X, y, test_size=0.2, random_state=42)
```

```
# Train model
model = RandomForestClassifier()
model.fit(X_train, y_train)
y_pred = model.predict(X_test)
print("Accuracy:", accuracy_score(y_test, y_pred))
```

Step 3: Evaluate Fairness

Check for disparities in approval rates across sensitive groups.

python

```
# Add predictions to test data
X_test['loan_approval_pred'] = y_pred
group_disparity                                    =
X_test.groupby('gender')['loan_approval_pred'].mean()
print(group_disparity)
```

Step 4: Apply Fairness Constraints

Use fairness-aware techniques to adjust model predictions.

python

```
from          aif360.algorithms.postprocessing          import
EqualizedOddsPostProcessing
```

```
# Apply equalized odds to adjust predictions
postprocessor = EqualizedOddsPostProcessing()
adjusted_predictions = postprocessor.fit_predict(y_test, y_pred,
sensitive_features=data['gender'])
```

Step 5: Monitor Post-Deployment

Regularly monitor model fairness and accuracy in real-world scenarios.

21.5 Analysis and Insights

1. **Expected Outcomes**:
   o Reduced bias in loan approvals while maintaining overall model performance.
2. **Challenges**:
   o Balancing fairness with predictive accuracy.
   o Dealing with limited or biased training data.
3. **Future Considerations**:
   o Continuous feedback loops for fairness improvement.
   o Publicly available fairness reports to maintain transparency.

This chapter explored the ethical challenges in deep learning, including bias, explainability, and fairness. By employing strategies like balanced datasets, fairness constraints, and explainability tools, practitioners can address these challenges effectively. The case study on loan approval models demonstrated how to identify and mitigate bias in a real-world application, underscoring the importance of ethical AI development. These principles ensure that deep learning models are not only powerful but also responsible and inclusive.

CHAPTER 22: FUTURE DIRECTIONS IN DEEP LEARNING

Deep learning continues to evolve rapidly, with emerging trends reshaping the field and introducing novel possibilities. Innovations like reinforcement learning and self-supervised learning are driving the next wave of breakthroughs, while advancements in quantum computing promise to redefine computational paradigms. This chapter explores these trends, the role of quantum computing, strategies for staying updated in this dynamic field, and culminates in a final project to build a complete NLP or vision system.

22.1 Emerging Trends in Deep Learning

22.1.1 Reinforcement Learning

Reinforcement learning (RL) trains models to make sequences of decisions by interacting with an environment and maximizing a reward signal. Unlike supervised learning, RL relies on trial-and-error exploration.

Applications:

- **Autonomous Vehicles**: Learning to navigate complex environments.
- **Gaming**: Mastering complex games like Go (e.g., AlphaGo).
- **Robotics**: Training robots to perform tasks in real-world scenarios.

Key Algorithms:

1. **Deep Q-Learning (DQN)**:
   o Combines Q-learning with deep neural networks to handle high-dimensional state spaces.
2. **Policy Gradient Methods**:
   o Learn directly the policy that maps states to actions.
3. **Actor-Critic Models**:
   o Combine value-based and policy-based approaches for improved stability.

Example Workflow:

- Define an environment (e.g., OpenAI Gym).
- Train an RL agent using a reward function.

22.1.2 Self-Supervised Learning

Self-supervised learning leverages large, unlabeled datasets by creating pretext tasks where labels are generated automatically from data. It bridges the gap between unsupervised and supervised learning.

Applications:

- **Language Models**: Models like BERT and GPT are trained on self-supervised tasks (e.g., masked language modeling).
- **Computer Vision**: Learning representations using contrastive learning techniques.

Key Techniques:

1. **Contrastive Learning**:
   - Encourages representations of similar data points to be closer in the latent space.
2. **Masked Modeling**:
   - Predict missing parts of input data (e.g., words in a sentence, pixels in an image).
3. **Transformers in Vision**:
   - Vision Transformers (ViT) adapt transformer architectures for image data.

22.2 Quantum Computing and Its Impact on Deep Learning

Quantum computing introduces a fundamentally different computational model, leveraging quantum bits (qubits) to perform computations exponentially faster for certain problems.

22.2.1 Potential Advantages

1. **Optimization Problems**:
   - Quantum algorithms like Grover's search can accelerate optimization tasks in neural network training.
2. **Quantum Neural Networks**:
   - Combine classical deep learning with quantum circuits for enhanced capabilities.
3. **Data Encoding**:
   - Process high-dimensional data efficiently using quantum states.

22.2.2 Current Challenges

- **Hardware Limitations**:
  - Quantum computers are still in their infancy, with limited qubits and high error rates.
- **Integration with Classical Systems**:
  - Bridging quantum and classical computation remains a complex challenge.

Future Outlook:

- Hybrid models combining quantum and classical techniques are likely to emerge as quantum hardware matures.

22.3 Tips for Staying Updated in the Field

Given the rapid advancements in deep learning, staying updated requires consistent effort and engagement with the community.

22.3.1 Learning Resources

1. **Research Papers**:
   o Read top conference papers (e.g., NeurIPS, ICML, CVPR) on platforms like arXiv.
2. **Online Courses**:
   o Platforms like Coursera, edX, and Udemy offer specialized courses.
3. **Books**:
   o Refer to foundational and cutting-edge texts on deep learning and AI.

22.3.2 Networking

1. **Conferences and Meetups**:
   o Attend AI conferences and local meetups to connect with researchers and practitioners.
2. **Social Media**:

o Follow AI leaders and organizations on platforms like Twitter and LinkedIn.

3. **Communities**:

   o Engage in forums like Reddit's r/MachineLearning and GitHub projects.

22.3.3 Hands-On Practice

- Regularly participate in Kaggle competitions.
- Contribute to open-source AI projects.

22.4 Final Project: Building a Complete NLP or Vision System

Step 1: Choose a Domain

1. **NLP System**:

   o Example: Build a chatbot, sentiment analysis tool, or machine translation system.

2. **Vision System**:

   o Example: Build an object detection model, face recognition tool, or image captioning system.

Step 2: Define the Project Scope

1. **Objective**:

   o Clearly define the system's purpose and expected outcomes.

2. **Dataset**:

- o Identify a dataset (e.g., IMDB for NLP, COCO for vision).

3. **Evaluation Metrics**:

- o Choose metrics to evaluate model performance (e.g., accuracy, F1-score, mAP).

Step 3: Develop the System
Example: NLP Chatbot

1. **Data Preparation**:

- o Preprocess conversational datasets (e.g., tokenization, lowercasing).

python

from transformers import AutoTokenizer

tokenizer = AutoTokenizer.from_pretrained('bert-base-uncased')
inputs = tokenizer("Hello, how can I help you?", return_tensors="pt")

2. **Model Training**:

- o Fine-tune a pre-trained transformer (e.g., GPT or BERT).

python

```
from transformers import AutoModelForSeq2SeqLM

model = AutoModelForSeq2SeqLM.from_pretrained('t5-small')
model.train()
```

3. **Deployment**:
   - o Deploy the model as an API using FastAPI or Flask.

Example: Vision System

1. **Data Preparation**:
   - o Load and preprocess the COCO dataset for object detection.

```python

from torchvision import datasets, transforms

transform = transforms.Compose([transforms.Resize((224, 224)), transforms.ToTensor()])
dataset = datasets.CocoDetection(root='coco/train2017', annFile='annotations/instances_train2017.json', transform=transform)
```

2. **Model Training**:

- o Fine-tune a pre-trained YOLO or Faster R-CNN model.

python

```
from          torchvision.models.detection          import
fasterrcnn_resnet50_fpn

model = fasterrcnn_resnet50_fpn(pretrained=True)
model.train()
```

3. **Deployment**:
   - o Serve predictions as a web application or mobile app.

Step 4: Evaluate and Optimize

1. Evaluate model performance using validation metrics.
2. Optimize for latency and accuracy.

22.5 Analysis and Insights

1. **Future-Proofing**:
   - o Stay agile and open to adopting new tools and methodologies.
2. **Collaboration**:

o Work with multidisciplinary teams to address ethical, computational, and domain-specific challenges.

3. **Scaling Innovations**:

o Leverage cloud and distributed systems for scalable solutions.

This chapter explored the future directions of deep learning, including reinforcement learning, self-supervised learning, and quantum computing's potential impact. Practical tips for staying updated in this fast-evolving field were provided, emphasizing the importance of continuous learning and collaboration. The chapter culminated in a final project, encouraging readers to apply their knowledge to build a complete NLP or vision system, embodying the principles and techniques learned throughout the book. These skills position you to tackle cutting-edge challenges and shape the future of AI.

www.ingramcontent.com/pod-product-compliance
Lightning Source LLC
LaVergne TN
LVHW051321050326
832903LV00031B/3285